THE GIRLFRIEND CHRONICLES
SECRETS, SKELETONS & STICKY SITUATIONS

MA'DESA KINCHLOW

CONTENTS

ACKNOWLEDGMENTS   i

1   LOVE DON'T LIVE HERE ANYMORE   Pg. 1

2   THINGS AREN'T AS THEY SEEM   Pg. 13

3   THE OTHER SIDE OF THE GAME   Pg. 20

4   SEEK AND YOU SHALL FIND   Pg. 29

5   THE SECRET IS EXPOSED   Pg. 34

6   DANGEROUSLY IN LOVE   Pg. 42

7   THE TRUTH SLAPS YOU IN THE FACE   Pg. 48

8   HERE WE GO AGAIN   Pg. 55

9   THE AFTERMATH OF HER VISIT   Pg. 60

10   HOW DID I END UP HERE   Pg. 65

11   IT'S TIME TO FIGURE THIS OUT   Pg. 72

12   SHOULD I STAY, OR SHOULD I GO   Pg. 82

13 RETURNING THE FAVOR   Pg. 90

14 HE'S PLAYING FOR KEEPS   Pg. 95

15 WHERE DO WE GO FROM HERE   Pg. 104

16 BACK TO REALITY   Pg. 110

17 CAUGHT RED HANDED   Pg. 116

18 CHOOSE YOUR WORDS WISELY   Pg. 125

19 SOMETIMES THE RIGHT THING TO DO IS HARD   Pg. 134

20 OUT WITH THE OLD…IN WITH THE NEW   Pg. 138

21 I'LL KEEP HOLDING ON   Pg. 143

22 THE TIME HAS COME TO LET GO   Pg. 148

23 ANOTHER ONE BITES THE DUST   Pg. 154

24 THE ROAD TO RECOVERY   Pg. 160

ACKNOWLEDGMENTS

First and foremost, I'd like to thank God for giving me a passion for and the gift of creating literary art. I'd like to thank my family and friends for their love, support, and encouragement during the process of making this dream a reality. You all are beyond appreciated! Last, but certainly not least, I'd like to thank my mother Sharon for all she has done to help me become a PUBLISHED AUTHOR! I did it Mama!

LOVE DON'T LIVE HERE ANYMORE (CHELSI ADAMS)

I arrived home stressed and exhausted from dealing with a bunch of disgruntled customers. There was a glitch in the computer system at the bank that caused thousands of customer's accounts to look like they had no money in their savings. I'd taken a ridiculous number of calls from several of my high balance customers who had threatened to pull all their money out if the issue was not resolved in 24 hours. It was a very long and stressful ass day.

I was glad to get out of that place and head to the sometimes-peaceful sanctuary of home. I hoped that my husband would be there and that maybe I could persuade him to talk. I knew that the chances of that happening were slim to none, because we were like two ships sailing in opposite ways; We barely talked and when we did attempt to communicate most of the time the simplest of conversations led to arguing. Things hadn't been good between us in a long time. It's sad that we must deal with stress at both work and home. We both work in the sometimes brutal and overwhelming corporate world. He is a high level executive account manager for a major marketing firm in the city of Indianapolis, and I am a personal banker with one of the largest banking institutions in the world. We don't have any children together, but I do have a son from a previous relationship. His name is Alex. He's 16 and he is the best kid. He is a great athlete and student. He lives in Ohio with his father. His father Jeff is a coach for one of the top private high schools in the entire state. They have one of the country's best high school basketball programs. I decided about two years ago to let Alex live with his father permanently. We had joint custody, but with he and I living in two different states it really made things hard for Alex. So, as hard as it was for me to let him go, I did the best thing for him and agreed to let him live with Jeff. He comes to visit on spring, summer, and holiday breaks…well that is if he doesn't have some sports camp or something to attend.

He plays Football, Basketball, runs Cross country, plays the snare drum, and the boy plays the piano. The kid has his father's talent and ambition in his blood. Jeff keeps him really busy because he is a good-looking boy and these hot in the ass little girls are always up in his face. He's already 6'0 ft tall and he weighs about 160lbs. He's built up just like Jeff. He is a perfect replica of him. Jeff often refers to him as his "mini-me". I know that he is a typical teenage boy and is interested in girls, but chances are if he is busy he won't have a lot of time to be somewhere laying up with a girl and make a slip up that could alter the course of his life forever. Some slip ups can take a life time to recover from. Let's face it, these kids now days are starting to have sex younger and younger. I just want my son to make sure that he doesn't repeat the same mistakes of his father and I.

Jeff and I were young and inexperienced. We didn't know anything about what it took to raise a child. We were for the most part still babies ourselves. Jeff gives him the facts. He is always very straightforward and blunt with Alex. I can appreciate his candidness, but sometimes I feel like he is too blunt. He himself is no stranger to the temptations and plight of the athletically talented boy becoming a man. He was an outstanding high school and college athlete. Basketball was his thing. He was great at it and I loved watching him play. Because of this, coupled with the fact that he was fine as hell, I stayed in some drama with some little fast ass girl trying to get him on her team. I'd vowed to myself to stay a virgin until marriage, but the pressure of others my age throwing their still maturing vaginas at Jeff caused me to rethink my choice.

We both had big dreams and never expected for our lives to change so dramatically right after high school graduation. We gambled and crapped out. I got pregnant with Alex a few months shy of graduation, but we both continued toward our dreams. A newborn yielded many sleepless nights and delayed plans. We were fortunate because we had the support of our families, so we were able to continue to work towards our life goals. We graduated college and subsequently have become pretty successful but, it wasn't easy. Jeff definitely had the talent and potential to go pro, but during a team scrimmage he tore his ACL and shattered his kneecap, and unfortunately his pro basketball career quickly ended before it ever began. It took him a really long time to accept the fact that he wasn't going to play ball, and this took a horrible toll on our already stressed relationship. So, I guess you can say that when the promise of his pro basketball career ended, so did our relationship. Jeff is a good-looking guy. He is the epitome of tall, dark, and handsome. His rich cocoa colored skin, that perfectly trimmed goatee, his jet black wavy hair, and those beautiful green eyes, mixed with that sexy Jamaican accent makes him quite popular with the ladies still till this day. He is a good father and he loves Alex and I am thankful that we have a really good relationship still; I appreciate Jeff, because with him there is no drama.

After a long day, the last thing that I needed was to come home to an argument. Quentin was obviously in one of his moods. I guess he'd had a bad day at the office and decided that he'd bring his nasty attitude home and share it with me. I walked into the kitchen from the garage to find him sitting at the table with his laptop open, him staring intensely at the screen. I studied his face and noticed the bags that were forming beneath his slanted, yet beautiful, brown eyes. I observed the wrinkles in his forehead and the look of pure exhaustion in his face. He looked frustrated and disconnected. I said "Hi Quentin! How was your day?" He didn't look up to even acknowledge me, and barely opened his mouth, saying, "What's up...it was cool."

I looked at him like he was crazy and thought to myself, oh no this mutha-fucka didn't! I wanted to snap, but I shook my head and walked away, burying my growing frustration. I entered our living room and stopped and glanced at the mantle over the fireplace. It was lined with pictures of our happier years. I couldn't help but be taken back to those days when it seemed as if Quentin loved me more than he loved anything. It was quite puzzling how we could go from being the happy couple, to the couple that barely even acknowledged each other.

We have been married for six years. Those pictures overflowed with the happiness that we once shared. The pictures captured and busted at the seams with the love that once ruled my heart. Now we are nothing more than roommates sharing space and walking on eggshells trying to keep the peace. We are married on paper and that's it. How I wished we could turn back the hands of time. I wished there was a way for me and my husband to rekindle the fire that made our marriage great once before, but it seems that we are too far gone.

I decided to go back into the kitchen; I walked over to Quentin and leaned over and kissed his cheek, then softly whispered in his ear, "I still love you. Why don't we have dinner tonight and talk about some things? What do you say?" He looked at me and shook his head as to say…girl you are crazy! He laughed and replied, "Chelsi I'm tired and I just want to rest. I'm not in the mood to talk. Maybe some other time."

I was irritated and continued to try and mask my frustration. I needed him to let his guard down because that was the only way I could get close to him. I got myself together and made my way upstairs to our beautiful master suite. We'd sure come a long way from the cramped, little two-bedroom apartment in downtown Indy. We now lived in a 5000 sq. ft. home in the city of Fishers. When we first got together we were in the process of paying off debt from college and didn't have a lot of extra money. We were both just scratching the surface of property management and it took a while to build some wealth, but we did it. We'd worked our way from the bottom and now are living a comfortable life.

I just wanted to forget about the day and relax in my big, beautiful, garden tub. I walked into bathroom and lit my vanilla scented aromatherapy candles that were lining the rear of the tub. I began to fill the tub and poured a little of my lavender and vanilla bath oil into the water to make it perfect to relax my tired, tension filled body. I turned on my cute, pink Bluetooth speaker and played my favorite playlist of R&B hits. I slid my tired body out of my clothes then stepped into the water. It was the perfect temperature to melt away the stress of the day and soothe me. I laid back as the powerful jets caressed my thighs.

After my bath, I walked out into my bedroom wearing an oversized bath towel. I heard the guestroom TV echoing off of the walls in the hallway and made my way to the doorway. I peeked in to find Quentin there. He seemed to be knocked out and resting comfortably on his back. I thought to myself that this would be the perfect time to put my plan into action. I momentarily stared at his beautiful body as he lay there scantily clad wearing nothing but a pair of black Polo boxer briefs.

To me, Quentin was all that and then some. His body was a work of art. A priceless Picasso. Damn, I forgot how fine he was! This man is a towering, solid, muscular dream. His body is ripped and right. He is one beautiful man! He has rich golden bronze colored skin, beautiful brown eyes, and he has the sexiest smile. His perfect facial features make him model material indeed. He looked so good and it was hard for me to resist the temptation to slide myself right into the bed and have my way with him. I knew that he was a hard sleeper and I could creep right into the bed with him unnoticed. I needed to make my move because with the way that things were going between us there was no guarantee I'd have another shot. It was now or never. It was do or die! I dropped the towel to the floor and slid my body into the bed next to Quentin. My hands moved meticulously across his body until I was holding every inch of his baby making package in my hands. I toyed with and manipulated it until it was standing at attention and ready for action. With him sleeping soundly, I mounted him and began to enjoy the ride. Operation "make a baby to recover my marriage" had begun.

He began to wake from his slumber and groggily moaned, "Chelsi, what are you doing? Come on now. What are you doing? You have to stop." I ignored him and methodically stirred my hips and clinched myself tighter around him and his tune quickly changed. He moaned, "Oooohhh shit! Damn girl!" His eyes rolled back into his head and I leaned down and kissed his lips. He opened his eyes and said in a breathy, yet euphoric fueled tone, "Chelsi we have to stop? You have to stop. Com'on now..."

I smiled and seductively purred, "Shhhhhhh, just let me take care of you. You know you've missed me. Just go with the flow. Trust me...we need this. You can't tell me this isn't what you needed." He continued to try to resist me, but his body was working against him. In his head he didn't want me, but his body had other plans. Then without uttering another word, he stopped fighting the urges from deep within and joined me in the quest for sexual satisfaction.

After finding himself lost and trapped in the sea of my body, he began to move more swiftly and deliberately. My body fell into submission and there we were fucking like two drunken strangers in the backroom of a hole in the wall nightclub. After finding himself lost in the moment, he finished his business and then hastily rolled out of the bed. He looked at me with a face of disgust and said, "I hope that you're happy! You got what you wanted Chelsi. It's too bad that you had to stoop as low as getting it while I was trying to rest. You never cease to amaze me!" He angrily walked into the bathroom of the guest suite and slammed the door, locking it behind him. I heard the shower running and sat there trying to figure out what just happened. It was crazy I felt like a whore. I was pissed! He was obviously having a regret filled, adult temper tantrum. This was not how this was supposed to go.

I jumped up out of the bed and began to beat on the door. I yelled, "What in the hell is wrong with you? How can you just fuck me and walk away like I'm some random bitch! I am your wife!". He snatched the door open and angrily yelled, "Chelsi, please stop with the bullshit. I woke up to you riding me! It wasn't like I pursued you! What did you expect me to do...stop? Don't fucking play the victim here! You didn't want me to stop! It's just what you wanted. You are foul for this shit! When is the last time I touched you? You can't remember, can you? Can you? No, you can't! We aren't a happy couple! We are like too roommates who share half of the mortgage and utilities! I don't even know why we are still together! We don't even talk! This is a marriage for show! So please don't pretend like this is something more than what it is!"

I walked closer to him and my heart was beating so hard and fast that it felt as if it was going to jump right out of my chest. I could feel the anger boiling over inside of me. I wanted to smack the shit out of his ass! I looked him in his eyes, and said, "You have a lot of nerve talking to me like you have lost your damned mind! How can you be ok enough to fuck me and then flip the script? That is some bullshit Quentin! What the hell is wrong with your ass? Who are you? You act like I'm a monster! You're not innocent! You wanted me! If you didn't you would have resisted and pushed me off of you. I was just woman enough to do what your lame ass wouldn't do….make a move!"

He held his head down and shook it side to side. He looked up with anger burning in his eyes. "I'm not doing this with you! Chelsi I can't deal with you right now! I gotta get out of here and clear my head!" He grabbed his clothes and I snatched them from his hands. I pulled him close and said. "Quentin, look baby, I'm sorry. I know you still love me! Let's work this out! I know we can. Didn't it feel amazing to be with me after all this time? We still have that magic! We can get back all of those feelings that made us great. Don't give up on us, please don't!" He said nothing, his face was filled with a look of anguish.

Still knowing that he was trying to get away from me I continued to pull him closer. I begged him to sit down on the bed. He bowed his head and sighed loudly as if I was getting on his last nerve. I tried to kiss him, and he pushed me away. He grabbed my arms and yelled, "Damn it Chelsi, please stop! This is not helping the situation!" He got up, dressed quickly and made his way to the door. I screamed his name and then burst into tears. He looked back, his face covered in momentary concern, and his eyes filling with tears of frustration. He turned and continued out the door.

Minutes later, I heard the sound of his car peeling down the street. My tears quickly turned to laughter and I sat there smiling deviously with my hand planted on my womb hoping that deep inside of me a new life was forming. My unsuspecting husband had no idea that earlier in the day I had confirmed that I was ovulating, and I wasn't interested in anything but making a baby. I couldn't lose my marriage and having a baby was my guaranteed insurance policy against divorce.

If I knew one thing about Quentin, he'd never walk away from his child even if that meant being miserable by staying with me. I was hopeful that my plan worked. I couldn't help but be happy that he unknowingly fell in line and played right into my hands.

Like many men, his big head lost the fight to his little head. I chuckled to myself...GOT EM! I needed to save my marriage because there was too much at stake. Don't get me wrong, I still had love for him, but there was too much time invested....and too much damned money tied up in this marriage! I couldn't let go. I was desperate, and I was using the best weapon that I had in my arsenal, myself.

THINGS AREN'T ALWAYS AS THEY SEEM
(KYRIA WILLIAMS)

Malcolm hurried in from the office yelling like an idiot, "Kyria! Where is my tux? Look, we have 45 minutes to get there!" I stood in the hallway giggling to myself with his tux in my hand. I swear this fool was going to have a stroke one day if his old ass did not stop going from 0 to 60 in 2.5 seconds. "Malcolm, I have everything right here! Just calm down! We're going to make it." He relaxed and then looked over at me and motioned for me to hand him the tux. I smiled and handed it to him. He then rudely said, "Where the hell is your dress? Why aren't you ready?" I knew that his calm and collected demeanor wouldn't last long. He was always so uptight. I played nice, and said, "Malcolm, please honey, I have to put my dress on, and I needed to finish feeding the baby. Joniece is here to watch him while we're out." He looked at me with a look of irritation and tried to muster up a smile. I tried not to laugh as he looked extremely pressed.

Malcolm was good looking, he was 15 years my senior but definitely didn't look his age. His bald head was actually kinda sexy. He had recently shaved it all off and I was glad because I didn't want him to be walking around with a "struggle fade". Malcolm and I had been together for a bit over two years. We were married only after three months of dating. I really wasn't ready to get married and wasn't really feeling Malcolm like that. However, girls like me from the hood weren't accustomed to successful, rich, entrepreneurs showing an interest in them. All the other guys that I dated were too busy playing games and I was tired of being toyed with.

I met Malcolm when I was temping at his office. He specializes in Commercial Real Estate Investing and the business has been good to him. Meeting him was right on time and just what I needed to get me out of my miserable, desperate situation of poverty and despair. My broke ass needed the come up. In the beginning, I made it a point to cater to his every need and be there at his every beck and call. I put it on his old ass something vicious a few times and he decided to wife me up. I went from rags to riches in no time.

One day I was eating a steady diet of beanie weenies, ramen noodles, and grilled cheese, and the next I was eating steak and lobster. I went from drinking $3.99 bottles of Boone's Farm to poppin bottles that cost $250 in VIP. We'd come from two totally different worlds and at times it was hard for me, but I adapted and went from the hood life I'd known, to high society life in an instant. I managed to fit in perfectly and no one knew I was born with a rusted spoon in my mouth instead of a silver one. Imagine going from a net worth of negative zero to a net worth of too many zeros to count. Don't judge me. My son Justin was born three months ago. He is my pride and joy. He is a little cutie, with curly, fine, cold black hair. His perfectly round head, and big bright hazel eyes makes him look like a cute little Cabbage Patch Doll. My son was the best thing that ever happened to me. He is the perfect baby and I am crazy about him. Malcolm never really spends much time with him and to think of it Malcolm doesn't spend much time with me either. He is always so consumed with work and money, that family comes last. This is often a point of contention in an already less than picture perfect marriage. Our sex life sucks, our communication sucks, our marriage sucks. I sometimes feel that he keeps me around to make himself look good. He's a control freak.

Malcolm is from a family of super chauvinistic men who believe women shouldn't work but stay home and care for the house and kids. I bet if his ass could keep me barefoot and pregnant he would. We haven't had sex in months and this is more often than not an issue for him because he expects me to drop my panties at his demand. To be completely honest, Malcolm doesn't have much respect for me as a woman or as a person. I feel like he holds his wealth and status over my head. He knows I come from nothing and am terrified to even think I'd be forced to go back there. It's difficult living with him, but I have learned to tolerate and accept his arrogant, snobbish attitude.

I guess you could say I deal with his mistreatment because I am living a life that I once only dreamed about. It feels good to spend money and not have to blink or even give it a second thought. The days of robbing Peter to pay Paul have been over for me since marrying him. We are very well off, and as long as I take care of the house Malcolm is going to take care of me.

My marriage isn't great and I really need more emotionally and physically, but as so many women do, I choose to suffer in silence and put up with his foolishness, because regardless of how much of an asshole he truly is, I want for nothing. I ride good, dress good, eat good, and for the most part I'm content. Well, I try to convince myself that I am.

Finally, after a few panicked minutes Malcolm was ready to go out the door. He was looking quite nice in his all black tux. He had on a crisp white shirt and a black bowtie that perfectly complimented it. I was to wear a mid-length, black, sequined, formal gown. Malcolm had it custom ordered for me from some upscale store in New York. He wanted me to look like a star; like I was on the red carpet. I am his young, pretty, trophy wife. Showing me off is something he's done with great pleasure.

So, I quickly donned my Spanx and slid into that $500 dress. In minutes we were walking out the door and heading to the limo parked outside. Malcolm instructed the driver to take us to the JW Marriott hotel downtown. We were attending a formal dinner party with all of the high society folks of Indianapolis and its surrounding cities. These "high society" parties never got old to Malcolm but for me I was too tired of them. I got sick of sitting around making senseless chatter with these snobby, stuck up bitches. The driver jumped on the freeway southbound, heading toward downtown Indy. As Malcom sat across from me, I noticed him scrolling through his I-phone. I knew he was working. It was always pretty quiet during our alone time. You'd think we'd be talking, but that rarely happened because he was always working. It was a little irritating at first, but I have gotten used to it and have stopped focusing on it because Justin keeps me so busy nowadays. I just sat there and scrolled through Facebook while waiting for us to arrive at the hot spot of the evening. We pulled in front of the Hotel and were escorted from the lobby to the lavish grand ballroom. It was beautiful. Crystal chandeliers, glass sculptures, gold and silver accented fixtures, deep dark colored wood and high-end decor gave the place a palatial feel.

We walked into the entrance of the room and Malcolm immediately started showing me off to all these high society folks. Some of them I'd seen at prior events and some of them were fresh faces, but I put on my trophy wife smile and made small talk with the other high society wives, mistresses, and girlfriends. I couldn't help but think about how much I missed kickin it with my girls Lissa, Tarah, and Shana. I sure miss their crazy asses. Malcom forbid me from hanging with my crew. He said I was on another level and I needed to forget about my "ghetto friends" and find me some friends in his circle, and like a dummy I stopped talking to them all! Damn, I can't believe I let this old ass fool alienate me from my friends.

After much mingling Malcolm spotted his new business partner JD. He and Malcolm had just teamed up to start a Venture Capital firm here in the city. I had overheard Malcolm talking about JD, but this was the first time we'd actually meet face to face. From what Malcolm said, JD commuted between here and Miami. He wasn't married, and was what Malcolm calls a "collector of fine women"; meaning that he never had the same woman on his arm. But surprisingly, tonight he was alone. We walked over to him, so Malcolm could introduce me. JD turned around and I thought I was going to die! I could not believe my eyes. I knew this man and he knew me as well. His face lit up like the sun and he looked at me with a deep, stern, yet sexy, unwavering stare and said, "Hello, Kyria, I've heard so much about you. It's a pleasure to finally meet you." I was a little shook, but I kept my shit together and replied, "Likewise JD, it's great to meet you." We stood there for a few seconds and there was this awkward silence. Malcolm asked JD to keep me company as he proceeded to mingle. I stood there looking around trying to avoid looking into JD's eyes.

He was a sight to see. I mean the total package, from top to bottom. He has the deepest, sexiest dimples and his smile was golden and seemed to light up the room. I marveled at the sight before my eyes, his perfect teeth, his high cheekbones, his fresh line up and his caramel brown skin was as smooth as silk. I was captivated by his beautiful amber brown eyes as they seemed to stare a hole straight through me. He was mysterious, and intriguing to me. I wanted badly to forget the memories of him that were consuming my mind but couldn't. I didn't know it, but my past was coming back to get me, and it was coming back relentlessly. I wasn't ready for this and I never could have imagined that in the next 24 hours my life was going to take a crazy turn, and the shit was literally about to hit the fan. I was going to find myself a character in a real-life Soap Opera.

THE OTHER SIDE OF THE GAME
(MARISSA KINCAID)

I jumped out of bed realizing that I had overslept. What the hell was I going to do? I had to get myself and three kids ready and try to make it to work on time. I hurried to the pink and purple painted wall, bedroom beside mine and yelled, "Bri and Ari get up! We are late!" I watched as my four-year-old twin girls rolled out of bed. I tried to rush them into the bathroom to wash their faces and brush their teeth. I went back into my room to see if the little "monster" was still sleep. His name is Brayden and he is my six-month-old terrorist child. That little boy is a busy body and a menace in a walker!

After making sure that he was still sleep, I went back into the girls' room and found them some clothes to wear. I grabbed two pairs of flare legged jeans with rhinestone covered pockets and two pink Hello Kitty shirts covered with cute sparkles. They raced to dress themselves. Brianna looked over at me and said, "Mommy, can you button this, I can't get it." I looked at her and said, "Yeah Bri Mama will do it." She smiled at me and I noticed that more and more she was looking like her father. Arianna ran over to me, pretending she had an issue as well. She looked at me and said with her crooked smile, "Mommy, I need your help please!" I laughed because I knew it was coming. Arianna was my little diva; the show stopper and she was always going to be the center of attention. It was amazing to me how my girls were identical, yet different. They looked the same, sounded the same, and even walked the same, but they possessed two totally different personalities. Brianna was more like me, quiet and reserved, while Arianna was more like their Dad, lively and full of energy. Sometimes I wished I could bottle up that energy and sell it, because I would be rich. I finished helping the girls and hurried to brush their hair into two cute little afro puffs. They have beautiful sandy brown hair that complements their rich golden toned skin. They are little sweethearts and I am proud to be their Mom. While finishing up the girls, I heard the familiar scream of Brayden's as he was waking from his sleep. This kid hated to wake up and every time cried like someone was trying to kill him. I ran into the room and grabbed him in my arms. He felt a little warm, so I decided to take his temperature. After about 30 seconds the thermometer, displayed 101.6. I was nauseous because I knew that meant I had to call into work today. I had tried to reach the kids father but had been unsuccessful. I sat in the middle of my bedroom floor and stared blankly at my peanut butter colored walls.

The kids' father wanted me to stop working, but I refused. He covers the rent and utilities, so I put my extra money in savings because I know that we are in an unconventional relationship and nothing is promised. I walked into the bathroom and opened the medicine cabinet; I gave Brayden some medication and yelled for the girls to come into the room. I told them that they needed to go into the kitchen and eat breakfast before their bus came.

I called into the call-in line for my job and had nervous butterflies in the pit of my stomach because my manager hates me. I tell you, she is a mean old hateful woman who claimed she is saved, but I swear that woman is as mean as a rattle snake. She is just nasty and for whatever reason, she is out to get me. The girls finished eating and soon it was time to send them to the door to wait for their bus. I laid Brayden down after rocking him to sleep and watched the girls as they sang little songs and played hand games, while waiting for their bus at the door. Brianna yelled, "Mommy here comes the bus!!" They ran to me and gave me big hugs and kisses and then ran outside to catch their bus.

After I got the girls off to preschool I sat in my lounge chair Indian style trying to figure out what I was going to do about my situation. I heard my phone ring a very distinctive tone, and I knew that it was one person...Robert, my "man" and father of my three children. Robert is a good man. He's loving, kind and has a great sense of humor. He handles his business. The man is definitely a go-getter. He's educated and down to earth. He has the perfect amount of street and book smarts to make it in this crazy world. He is a natural born hustler and just knows how to make it happen. He has so much talent and drive. I admire his ambition and his generosity. He is easy on the eyes and is undoubtedly a charmer. He never minds doing anything for me, or for anyone else for that matter. He is always somewhere giving back to the community, and I love that about him. I know he'd give me the world if I asked. He just recently bought me a new SUV for my birthday. It is a fully loaded 2017 Lexus GX. It is Metallic Silver and I love it!

He and I met after my relocation from Phoenix, Arizona. I moved here after my father suddenly passed away from a massive stroke. I never knew my mother because she died shortly after I was born from complications of childbirth. My father raised me alone with the help of my aunts and late grandparents.

I moved here because I needed a change. I was sick of my Aunts trying to marry me away to every eligible bachelor in the church house. I had an old friend from school who had moved to Indy and she had nothing but remarkable things to say, so I decided to take a chance.

One evening Robert came by to help me with an issue I was having at the house and we started talking. Minutes became hours and it was like we were drawn to and completely understood one another. Our innocent, casual conversation turned into something more and that night I found myself exchanging love faces with another woman's husband, and here we are some years and three kids later in this mess. After learning of my affair, my Aunts back in Arizona disowned me. They told me that I was a horrible person and that they wanted nothing to do with me or my "sinfully" born children.

Yeah, you guessed it. They are bible toting, scripture quoting, super judgmental church ladies with big ole hats who seem to believe that this an unforgivable sin, and that I'm unredeemable. It's amazing how so many of us good Christian folk will pick and choose what sin we deem as unforgivable concerning another, but we expect God to forgive us for all that we do. I know that my situation is frowned upon, and I don't expect anyone to be sympathetic to me or ever attempt to understand, but in my mind, them treating me like I don't exist and damning me to hell makes them no better than me. What happened to loving others with the love of Christ?

I was raised in the church and was taught to avoid the very thing that has become a struggle in my life. Who would have thought the preacher's daughter would be involved in a scandal such as this? God knows I never intended for this to be my life, but I guess the truth of the matter is that, no one is exempt from falling into the temptation of sin. Sometimes we fall and once we've landed in the pit we have a very difficult time pulling ourselves out. I'm thankful daily because I don't deserve his mercy.

When I learned of my pregnancy I felt so ashamed and secretly prayed that I'd miscarry because I didn't want to deal with the guilt of being pregnant by a married man. I could not have an abortion because I would never be able to forgive myself for taking life in my own hands. I hid my pregnancy from Robert for five months and was making plans to leave the city unnoticed. One day he popped up unannounced and discovered that I was pregnant. He asked if the baby was his and I told him yes, and it was twin girls. So that's how we happened. Here I am, alone, with no family here, in love with a married man.

Despite our situation Robert takes great care of us. We have whatever we want and need. The girls are his little princesses. They love him, and he is a superhero to them. He adores them and spoils them rotten. With Brayden, he is like any other man with their son. He's proud of his boy. He sits Brayden on his lap and talks to him about sports. Sometimes they fall asleep in the lounge chair watching ESPN Sports Center. It's so cute to see Robert laid out and Brayden lying across his chest, they look just alike when sleeping. Loving Robert isn't easy but letting him go would be much harder. I know it's not anything to be proud of, but this is my life.

I answered the phone with an attitude. His deep voice responded on the other end, "Hey what's going on with you baby? How are my kids?" With a sour face and a flat tone, I answered, "Well maybe you'd know if you'd come and see them! Where have you been? I've been calling you for three days Robert!" He sighed and said, "Look calm down, I had to take some time and think some stuff through. I am really dealing with some shit right now. I took a little trip to handle some stuff and I lost my damned phone when I went to the casino. Look, baby-girl, I just got my phone back today and that's why I was calling to check in. I'm sorry baby, don't be mad at me."

I swear I wanted to believe him, but my mind was racing. There were so many thoughts running through my head. Was he with someone else? Did he decide to patch things up with his wife? Was he off playing the good husband while I was sitting here stressed out and tired with his kids? I sat there stewing and said, "Whatever Robert! What's up? Look, Brayden's sick and I had to call in." He quickly cut me off saying, "Aww man my boy is sick? I'm coming right over. I was going to come after work, but I'm headed there now baby. I miss you and the kids, and I also have to drop this money off that I promised to give you. Unlock the door, because I left my keys in my truck. I'll see you in 10."

I said "Whatever." and hung up the phone. As soon as I hung that phone up I skipped my happy ass into the bathroom and made sure that I was looking presentable. I hated our situation, but I loved Robert and I wanted to make sure I looked good to him at all times. I brushed my auburn brown naturally curly locks into a cute, messy ponytail and slipped on some blue yoga pants and one of Robert's white tees that he'd kept in his drawer for the nights he stayed here. I looked in on Brayden and went downstairs and tried to act as if I was doing something. I knew that Robert's ten minutes was going to be 30. I studied the clock and noticed that it was nearing 25 minutes and there was still no sign of him. I returned upstairs to my bedroom and laid across my bed.

My stomach was churning from disappointment; I closed my eyes and dozed peacefully into a little nap. That little cat nap was rudely interrupted as the sensation of ice cold hands ran across my lower back. I was startled, yet excited. The cold hands were followed by soft kisses to my neck, I turned, and it was Robert. "Hey Big Booty Judy...did you miss me?" I chuckled, and shook my head no, and he said, "Yes you did, and this is how I know!" He grabbed my face and kissed me passionately. His kisses were warm, wet, tasty, and entrancing. Damn, it felt so good to feel his lips on mine and as bad as I hated him for making me his illegitimate "baby's mama". I loved him too much to resist him. I loved him too much to walk away from him. I loved him too much to make him stop. He then took my body captive with his touch and with every inch of his manhood and I didn't want to be freed.

SEEK AND YOU SHALL FIND
(CHELSI ADAMS)

Days had passed since Quentin angrily left the house. I called his phone several times and it went straight to voicemail. I was a little worried, but I knew that Quentin would often turn his phone off or block my number when he was upset and didn't want to be bothered. He would never do that for days on end though. I hoped that he'd make it home soon, because I really needed to talk to him and try to get his guard down some more. I was determined to play the role of the heartbroken wife grieving the relationship, in the hopes that I'd trick him into giving it to me again because of his guilt. One thing I know for sure is that he enjoys sex and I know all the tricks to get him where I need him. I had to get pregnant.

Quentin said that he didn't want children; we'd tried some years back and lost our son early in the 2nd trimester. That loss devastated him, because he had emotionally invested so much so early into the pregnancy. It played a huge part in the breakdown of our marriage because I wanted to immediately try again, and Quentin refused. He said that he would not have sex with me without protection. He asked me to take the pill again, and I agreed because I didn't want to lose my husband. I know the shit is crazy, but I did what I needed to do to keep my man, or so I thought. My mama always told me that what I wouldn't do, some other woman would. It seemed that when the baby died part of our marriage died with him. We never really seemed to get back on track.

I tried to call Quentin again and finally after about seven calls he answered the phone! "Quentin, where are you? I've been calling you for days! We really need to talk!" He said "Hey, I'm sorry, I had to take a trip last minute to settle some business; I didn't feel that it mattered to you that I'd be gone. I will be back in a few days. I been fighting through the airport traffic and trying to make these last-minute arrangements. I can't talk right now Chelsi. I will talk to you when I get back…I have to go." Then there was silence followed by the annoying echo of the dial tone. Who does that? Who goes on a business trip without telling their wife? I know that we are not in a good place, but damn! Anything could happen, and I'd be the last to know. I was so angry that I wanted to cry, but I needed to keep myself as emotionless and as rational as possible because I was on a mission.

I went into the workout room and started to run on the treadmill. I was hoping to run my frustrations away but stopped suddenly. I was praying that deep inside of my body a life was forming. I know that it was shady and wrong of me to trick my husband into having sex with me to get pregnant, but desperate times called for desperate measures. I was desirously craving that the aftermath of the deceitful encounter would yield a result of a baby. I needed this baby because I needed to save my marriage, and I wasn't going to stop until I got what I wanted. I was in a war and I had to win it. After stopping my workout, I decided to do some reorganizing in the house.

I went upstairs to Quentin's office to make sure his mini fridge was stocked with his favorites. He wasn't a big drinker, but every once in a while, he loved to kick back watch a game of football or basketball and drink a beer or two. I figured that he'd appreciate the gesture and unharden his heart. I walked around his office and noticed how dusty it was, so I decided to do a little cleaning. I opened the door to the storage closet looking for some dusting cloths. I grabbed the box from the top shelf and a medium sized, brown interoffice envelope fell to the floor and some of its contents spilled out. As I gathered the papers, my curiosity was peaked.

I sat in the middle of the walk-in closet floor debating on whether or not to invade my husband's privacy by going through the paperwork. I knew I was dead wrong, but I had to find out what all was in that envelope and more importantly why it was hidden in the closet.

I hesitantly flipped through the contents of the envelope and found a receipt for baby items. These items were delivered to our rental property some months ago. My stomach churned from the fear of what else I'd find. The thought of what I'd find on the next document in queue terrified me. I was not ready and nothing could have prepared my eyes for the shit I was about to see. The sickness in the pit of my stomach cautioned me to stop, but I needed to keep digging. My inner detective had been awoken.

I flipped to the next piece of paper and there it was plainly in my face! It was a copy of a child's birth certificate listing my mutha-fuckin husband as the father! The name of the mother listed was the bitch who lived in my rental property! All kinds of thoughts rushed through my head. My mind was a tornadic storm of confusion and fury. The rage that was inside of me was reflected in my face. My nostrils flared like a raging bull ready to slaughter its taunting matador! I saw nothing but red. I dialed Quentin and the phone went straight to voicemail. Then it dawned on me! I didn't have to wait for him I was going to go to her! I knew where this whore lived. She lives in my investment, and I'm going to pay her a visit! She's going to tell me everything and I wasn't leaving until I knew it all. Even if I needed to beat her ass, I was going to get answers. I was so angry I could kill. I was out for blood. I ran and put on my shoes, grabbed my purse and keys and jumped into my car, headed straight to the little whore that had been fucking my husband. I left my home, ready to swarm on that bitch but I did not know that my life was about to come crashing down!

THE SECRET IS EXPOSED
(KYRIA WILLIAMS)

After two hours at that long dinner party I was tired and ready to go home. I missed my baby, and I know he missed me too. I motioned to Malcolm to come over; he was busy talking business and politics. I said, "Malcolm I'm ready to go home. I'm tired and I miss Justin." He responded, "Kyria we can't leave right now! You have to wait until I'm done!" I hated when he took that tone with me. I could tell by the wrinkles in his forehead and the way he was biting his bottom lip that he was irritated as hell. He looked over and motioned for JD to come over.

JD's sexy ass walked over, and I nearly lost my balance, and started drooling. Malcolm said, "Hey man, are you leaving?" JD answered, "Yeah man I'm calling it a night I need to head home and get packed. I have to fly to Miami in the morning." Malcolm replied, "Well look man can you take the little lady home for me because she's a little tired and it looks like this is going to be a long night." JD shook his head yes and said, "Kyria are you ready?" I reluctantly said yes.

I kissed my husband goodbye and walked out the door, ready to face my past head on. JD held the door of the hotel open and motioned for the valet to bring him his car. In minutes his sexy, royal blue, shiny, BMW was sitting there. It was a real beauty. JD opened the door and I sat in the car. It smelled like it was brand new. He tipped the valet driver and shook his hand. He closed the door and fastened his seatbelt, and said, "Are you ready to go?" I nodded yes, and we were on our way.

There was dead silence and I couldn't take it any longer. I said, "JD, you know who I am…. why are you here? What kind of sick game are you playing?" He said, "Yes, Kyria, how could I forget the woman who broke my heart in Miami." I looked at him still trying to digest the truth; of him being here in the flesh.

How and the hell did this happen? Who would have guessed I'd be looking at him? Jayson Davis was his name and he was the man that I had an affair with over a year ago when I took a break from Malcolm and went to Miami for two weeks. He and I had met on the beach and it was an instant attraction. He was my type. Tall, and muscular. His body was perfect, and he had the sexiest dimples and smile to match. His eyes roped me in at hello. They were the most beautiful amber brown that I'd ever seen, and he was such a gentleman. This man was the truth, and he and I seemed to click immediately. We walked and talked for hours. We sat watching the sun come up over the oceans reflective floor. I felt as if I could be with him forever. He seemed to be the perfect man. He was different than any other man I had ever met and for the first time ever in my life, I wanted a man that I barely knew. I wanted him, and I wanted him real bad.

Even though our introduction was only nearing 24 hours old, it didn't matter because the feeling of infatuation and attraction was mutual. We spent two weeks having the time of our lives. My mornings began with us making love on the private balcony of his beachfront condo and my nights were concluded the same way. I was in bliss and I failed to mention to him that I had a husband waiting on me in Indianapolis. He was exciting and fun, and I didn't want to leave him, but I needed to. My last night there I couldn't dare leave without telling him the truth; I had to let him know that our time was over. I devastated him. He felt hurt because I'd lied to him but more hurt because I belonged to someone else and he wanted me for himself. We were that once upon a time, love at first sight phenomenon that we've all heard and read about in love stories. I left his home that night and never looked back.

I returned to my life in Indianapolis, Miami was over. We were over. I thought he would just remain a sweet memory, but here he was in the flesh.

He drove me to my house and he asked if we

could talk for a while. I cautiously agreed, and we walked into my house. I told him to have a seat. I walked into the family room and Joniece was sitting there watching TV. I paid her and told her thank you. She said that Justin was such a good baby and she'd thanked me for letting her sit with him. I walked her to the door and she waved goodbye and she got into her cute, little, cherry red sports car and drove away into the darkness of the night.

I walked back and had to face JD and resolve whatever this was before my husband came home. I needed to make sense of this madness. I had to find out why he was here. Is it possible that he knew my secret? How could he? I sat across from him holding on tightly to my little secret. My cell phone rang, and it was Malcolm. "Hey Malcolm, what's up?" He answered, "Look I'm going to hang here and talk business for a little while longer, please don't wait up. I figured you were home already, JD told me that he dropped you off." I said, "Ok well, be safe and I'll see you later." I was irritated, and I guess that JD could see it in my face and asked if I was alright. I shook my head yes and asked if he'd excuse me for one moment.

I returned moments later cradling Justin. He then asked, "How old is the baby?" I said, "He's two months old." He smiled and told me that he was beautiful. I wanted to scream.... I wanted to tell him that Justin was his child, but I couldn't. I couldn't tell him that finding him was something I didn't want to do. It was something that I couldn't do because if I revealed to my husband that I had an affair and that our baby was another man's, I'd lose everything. Things would get real if I would have shared my secret, and I couldn't and wouldn't take the chance. There was too much uncertainty. I didn't know how to find him and what if he didn't want a child? It was safer for me to just live life with Malcolm. I wouldn't take the chance of being broke again. I looked at JD and he looked at me. He grabbed my hand and said, "Listen, I haven't stopped thinking about you one day since you left Miami. I dream about you, I can still feel you, smell you, and taste you."

Glaring at me deeply he continued, "I know that you and I met for a reason and I came here to recapture what we had. Look, I'm not being arrogant, but I can have any woman that I want but I choose you. I know that Malcolm is your husband, but I know you don't truly love him. He doesn't satisfy you the way I did. He doesn't treat you like a man should treat a woman. You aren't happy. Don't even try to convince me that you are. There is no way a woman who was happy in her marriage and being fulfilled could make love to me the way you did for two weeks. I know you feel this connection and truthfully I bet you are glad that I am here." I snatched my hand away from his and said, "You don't know what the hell you are talking about! It was a fling! It was a one-time sexual rendezvous in beautiful Miami. My life is here with Malcolm and my son! You have a lot of nerve coming here with this delusional mess! I want you to leave!...NOW!" He grabbed my hand again and said, "Kyria, you mean my son? I did the math...that baby is mine...isn't he?" I didn't respond but lowered my head in shame and walked away to place my now sleeping son in his bassinet.

I returned to the living room, still not responding to JD. He just kept pushing, and after one look into his eyes it was over. I admitted to JD that Justin was in fact his child. I learned of my pregnancy 6 weeks after arriving home. He looked relieved to know the truth and honestly, I felt a bit relieved myself. Harboring a secret of this magnitude takes a toll on you both physically and mentally. JD began to speak, and I listened as he told me of his sadness when I walked out of his life. My heart was quickly unhardened by the reality that this man actually cared for me and had come to find me. As he talked I realized how much I truly missed what we had shared in Miami. I didn't have that here with Malcolm. It had been over a year since I felt the way that he made me feel. I found myself reliving the moments in Miami. Deep down inside there was a part of me that was wishing to revisit them. What the hell was I thinking? I had to be out of my mind. I stared into his eyes once more and I felt my body begin to betray me. I could tell by the look in his eyes that his body was betraying him too. There was something about this man's eyes that cast a spell on me.

His eyes stared at me and pierced a hole straight through me once more. I leaned forward and before you know it my lips were glued to his. My tongue was overtaken by the wavelike force of his and I was helpless and under his control. He pulled me closer and began to touch me softly. He was so careful and considerate with his hands, as he had been those many times before in Miami. With each touch he further convinced my body to continue in its betrayal of me. He slid his hand up my dress and found my treasure spot. His fingers danced within the pulsating sea of my love. As he toyed with my body shocks of power shuddered through to my core. Damn! There was no turning back now. He pulled me on top of him and before you know it, we were naked on the couch and he had once more invaded the confines of my most secret and sacred place. I lay there unable to feel past the pleasure that he was giving me. He kissed and touched me in a way that said that he truly missed me. This night he was making his presence known. He touched my soul. His body became a heat seeking missile and weapon of love.

Before I could regroup from the force of him, he'd come back with another powerful blow, launching himself deeper and deeper until my body lost control and I stopped trying to fight the inevitable release of my liquified emotions...all over him. Tears flooded my eyes and trickled down my cheeks. I was in oblivion and not intending to, I yelled his name and told him I loved him and begged for more and more.

He accepted my request and we continued our quest to recreate the multiple orgasmic condo balcony scenes of before. Then after a few emotionally charged exchanges of words he roared and grunted, groaned and moaned and I knew by the stiffness of his body that he'd released all of his biological passion and fury within me. He kissed me tenderly and said, "Kyria we belong together, I love you, please come back to me." Tears continued to stream down my face as we laid there in the aftermath of our infidelity. My secret was out and there was nothing that I could do about it. I knew that JD wasn't going to go away quietly. How was I going to tell my husband? He was an asshole and I was miserable, but he didn't deserve this. No one deserves this.

DANGEROUSLY IN LOVE
(MARISSA KINCAID)

I woke from a nap and went downstairs. I saw Robert stretched out on the floor with the girls sitting on his back. Brayden was sitting in his walker while Robert was spinning him from side to side. Brayden chuckled and his cute little laugh caused Robert and the girls to fall over in a fit of laughter of their own. It was great to see my kids and their father having a good time. I walked closer and said, "Hey guys!" The girls ran and showered me with plenteous hugs and kisses. Arianna's face was covered in a huge toothy grin as she said, "Guess what Mommy? Daddy is gonna stay here at our house! He said he don't have to go to his work for three days and he is gonna be over our house the whole time! He's gonna make us pancakes and let us ride on his back! He's gonna stay for 50 hundred hours Mommy!" I chuckled at her enthusiasm and dramatic flair. Then Brianna chimed in saying, "And guess what else Mommy? Daddy is gonna sell his other big house and get a new house by the water for us to live in. He showed us the pictures, and me, Ari and Bray-Bray have our own room! He said we can paint our walls yellow! He is getting us a tree house castle in the backyard, and he said that we can have a pool with a waterslide!" I stood there and admired the fact that my girls were beaming with pride and joy. I hoped that he wasn't selling my daughters an unattainable dream as my Father had sold me in my youth.

My father meant well, but nothing ever worked out the way he said it would. He promised me a Mother for years when I was a little girl, but I was never fortunate enough to get more than a view of Sister "so-and-so" creeping out of his bedroom in the wee hours of the morning. It was one thing that my Father never made happen. I'm sure that he intended and hoped that one of his not so under the cover relationships with his many female church members would produce something more than a late-night creep into his bedroom after Wednesday night Bible Study, but he died a lonely widower with nothing more than a few hundred dollars in his savings and his prized brown leather-bound bible.

Robert looked up at me and said, "Com'on baby, sit down with us and take a look for yourself." I looked at a picture of a huge, luxury home in Geist. It was beautiful and at the bottom of the page the listing price was more than anything I'd ever seen. I flipped through the pages and found myself lost in a daydream, imagining myself and Robert meeting with interior designers working hard to make the house a home. I thought to myself, Oh my God! It was true, he is buying a house for me and the kids! We really were going to be a family just like he said! He's going to fulfill his promise. It was soon time for the girls to go to bed; while I was sleeping Robert had fed and bathed them. He'd even fixed Brayden's bottles for the night and had them ready for him in the cooler on the table next to his crib. I was amazed by his actions; It seemed that he was trying to get himself prepared to be a full-time dad. I went and kissed the kids goodnight. Robert sat comfortably in their room reading them their favorite bedtime story. I couldn't help but find myself falling more and more in love with this man.

Even though Robert wasn't the perfect man and we were in a really fucked up situation, no one could ever take away from him the fact that he was a good father to his kids. He loved them so much and I knew that no matter what happened with us, he'd never turn his back on his babies. I walked into my bedroom and decided to take a shower. I took my hair down, took my clothes off and stepped into the shower. I was humming and just letting the water dance down my back. I closed my eyes and concentrated on the wonderful feeling of the water beating down on my skin.

After about 20 minutes, I stepped out soaking wet from head to toe but feeling refreshed and revived.

It felt good not to have to do anything but relax and watch TV. I walked out of the bathroom to find Robert sitting on the edge of the bed. There were candles lit and soft music playing. The bed was covered with fresh rose petals. In his hand was a bottle of massage oil. He motioned for me to come closer and instructed that I stand in front of him. I obliged him and stood there in front of his face. He loosened my towel and began to caress my body, with his hands that were drenched with the sensual massage oil.

The tasty smell penetrated my nostrils and my body continued to delight in the touch from the strong hands of my sexy lover. He laid me down massaged every part of my body and I found myself going to sleep. I was so relaxed. I was lying on my stomach enjoying every minute of this pampering. Suddenly I felt the weight of his body on top of mine. He whispered in my ear and told me that he loved me. He told me that he wanted to make things right for me and our kids. He asked me if I'd consider marrying him when things were settled with him and his wife and I said of course. He rolled to his back and pulled me on top of him. He wrapped his strong arms around me and just held me tightly; we dozed into a peaceful sleep but were suddenly awakened by Brayden's crying. I started to get up and Robert stopped me, "I got him baby you just rest!" He finished tending to Brayden and by this time I was groggier than ever. I was almost drifting away into slumber land when he slid back into the bed. He proceeded to wrap me up in the warmth of his body. He began kissing me and touching me like he was trying to tell me something.

My back was facing his chest and I could feel the beginning of his body reacting to the urge within that we were both feeling. He whispered in my ear, "Can I have you forever?" I nodded yes, and we began the process again of consummating our new commitment to one another. Robert was different that night. His touch was gentler, his kiss sincerer. He slowed his motion and took his time exploring every part of me. He continually told me that he loved me and that I felt amazing. It was as if he was falling in love with me all over again. With each stroke I found myself falling deeper and deeper into the reality of our life. I held him tightly and wished that he'd stay camped and hidden within me for the rest of the night.

I rearranged my body and begin to taste the sweetness of his lips. He continued to dance circles within the depths of me. He and I both were on our way to the fireworks and explosions felt from intense, yet forbidden love and lustful satisfaction. I braced myself for the power packed biological punch that his body was giving me. I held on tightly with each earth-shattering motion, delighting in everything that he was serving. We were there together. I wanted to scream, but I didn't want to wake the kids, especially Brayden. Robert laughed at me because he knew I was trying to mask my screams, he pushed harder and whispered in my ear.

"I love you Marissa. I promise to make things right. Please trust me." Tears invaded my eyes and flowed swiftly. I realized that he was all that I needed and wanted, no matter how twisted our life. We laid there basking in the heat of our love making session. He kissed me deeply and held me closely. I listened to his heartbeat and watched as his chest rose and fell. I snuggled closely beside him and drifted off into peaceful paradise with my lover...my children's father...another woman's husband.

THE TRUTH SLAPS YOU IN THE FACE
(CHELSI ADAMS)

I pulled up outside the rental condo in Castleton. I immediately spotted Quentin's car in the driveway. I didn't deal with the day to day business concerning our rentals. Quentin was the one who handled maintenance issues and any concerns related to our tenants. I only dealt with the finances. I never had an issue with it. I had asked Quentin why he had not been collecting rent from this tenant and he said, she'd fallen on tough times, so he decided to let her stay rent free for a while because we did not need the money. It all makes perfect sense now. He's been sleeping with this woman for months while pretending to be a saint! Here I thought he was helping a person in need by allowing her to stay rent free, but the only helping he was doing was helping himself to a new piece of ass. Apparently, he is not just generous with money and assets, but he is also generous with that which hangs between his legs. I figured that he had stopped over to see the baby and had her take him to the airport.

I decided that I wasn't going to act a fool. I was going to be an adult. I was going to step to her and talk to her like a grown woman, besides I was too old to be fighting over a man! I got out of the car and walked slowly to the door. The porch light was on but there wasn't a single light on in the place. It was close to 10 and I figured that she was probably in bed with her child. I knocked on the door and a few moments later I noticed that a light came on, so I knew that the hoe was coming to answer. I heard a crying baby, and when the door opened I was stunned. Standing there in a wife beater and basketball shorts was my husband Quentin. He was holding a little baby boy. This was undoubtedly his son, he was a spitting image of him.

We both stood there momentarily speechless. Looking like he'd seen a ghost, he finally said, "Chelsi! What are you doing here?" I was pissed, and screamed, "I should be asking you the same thing you lying bastard! You've been fucking this bitch! She is your side bitch and baby's mama! I found the fucking birth certificate and receipts from the baby store! You've been playing house with this trick and I want to know how long this shit has been going on!" At that exact moment I lost it all! I didn't want to adult anymore and I wasn't going to play nice! Quentin's little whore came running to the door behind him, and said, "Robert, what's going on? Is everything ok? Who is she?"

I flipped completely out and said "No you stupid

bitch everything is not ok? Who am I? I'm the wife hoe! I'm your other landlord! The one that approved your application!" I smirked and looked at Quentin's ass and chuckled. "What kind of game are you playing? You have this little bitch calling you by your middle name? Explain to me how you were just laying up with me a few days ago and how now you're here? Just two weeks ago, you were doing all that talking about being sorry, and wishing you could turn back the hands of time. You got that right you are sorry! You're a pathetic, weak, cheating, lying bastard! You ain't shit!" I could see that the little thot was taken back by what I said, but still tried to act unbothered. She wouldn't give me the satisfaction of showing her hurt. The little side piece must have got tired of being a bunch of bitches and looked at me like she was tough, and yelled, "Look chick! You have one more time to call me a bitch and I'm gonna show you how much of a bitch I am!"

My face exploded in laughter and I replied, "Whatever BITCHHHHHHHHHHHH! What are you gonna do?" Quentin turned to her and yelled, "Marissa, take the baby and I will handle this." She started to argue, and he screamed, "Marissa! Take the baby and get in the fucking house now!" She grabbed the baby, looked at me and rolled her eyes as tears began to fall from them. I poked at her again, "Yeah, do as you're told little girl and go in the house before you get your ass beat!"

She walked away, and I knew she was on fire inside. She wanted to say something, but he had her in line, so she wouldn't dare say anything else. Quentin looked at me disgusted. "Chelsi, what the hell is wrong with you? This is not the time or the place for this shit! How in the hell are you going to come over here starting shit! Your problem is not with her! It's with me! Now, leave before you wake my daughters up!" After he said that, his face went as pale as a ghost once more as he realized that he had just told on himself big time! From the look on my face he knew that I didn't know that there were other children. This nickel slick, cheating son of a bitch had been playing house with this woman for years and had a whole family right under my nose.

What kind of Days of Our Lives, Young and The Restless bullshit was he pulling? I screamed, "What the hell do you mean leave before I wake up your daughters! Your daughters? Your daughters? What the fuck do you mean your daughters?" I was seething with an enormity of hatred. "You raggedy bastard how could you do this to me. I knew that you would probably end up screwing around on me because things weren't good, but you've got an entire family with this hoe! I asked you for children and you refused me, now I know why!" He looked at me and said, "Look Chelsi, I'm sorry. It has been over for us a long time. I never intended for things to go this way. There was a time that I wanted to try and fix our marriage, but that was a long time ago! I got here with my kids and I realized that this is where I needed to be. We are beyond repair and there is nothing left to say or do. If you'd be honest with yourself, you know that I am telling the truth. I promise I never wanted you to find out this way, but look I filed for divorce this morning! I'm sorry, I didn't mean to meet Marissa and fall in love. You were so cold after we lost the baby, and she just happened to be there. We made a mistake and slept together one time and eventually it became something more. She got pregnant and I knew that you couldn't handle that. When she got pregnant with the girls I couldn't bring myself to tell you. We were fighting all the time! You never talked to me or made me feel needed. It was like the only thing you wanted me for was to get you pregnant. You lost interest in me and gained interest in my seed only! There were times that you just wanted to have sex and you didn't respect me as a man. You lost respect for my feelings. I'm not saying that this is right, but it took two of us to make this marriage fall apart. Chelsi you focused on yourself and forgot about me! I hurt too when we lost our son, but you were too selfish to think about me. You stopped being my wife and stopped caring all because I didn't want to have a baby! You treated me like shit!"

I snapped! "What the hell do you mean I treated you like shit? You were my husband! We were supposed to have a family! The family you have with this bitch is the family you were supposed to have with me! I am your wife! You knew how much I wanted that baby! You knew how long we had tried to conceive! You knew that it was a huge blow to my confidence as a woman when I lost that baby! I knew how much you wanted him! I wanted to give you another one! I knew we could have another one! You just gave up and I wasn't ready to give up! So please stop with the woe is me act. You aren't a battered, broken man! So don't you dare try to make this my fault! You're a sorry excuse for a man who obviously has trouble keeping that below average sized penis in your pants! You've got a lot of nerve standing here like I did something so awful that warranted you having an affair and starting an entire new family with another woman! I swear you aint shit!"

Suddenly one of the little girls ran to the door and yelled with her eyes drowning in tears. "Daddy please don't go you said you were gonna stay here…why is the Lady mad at you? You said we was gonna go to our new house by the water! Please daddy me and Ari promise to be good we promise to pick up our toys and eat our peas…please Daddy don't go away again!" She started crying hysterically holding onto his leg. Quentin knelt down and grabbed her up in his arms. He wiped her tears and softly replied, "Brianna, baby, Daddy isn't going anywhere. I promise. Now, please be a big girl and just go inside with Mommy and help her with Bray-Bray." The other little girl ran out and said, "Daddy, Mommy is crying, and she won't stop! Bray-Bray is crying and saying da-da, he's saying da-da, so Daddy you have to come and get him."

He looked at me and said, "Please Chelsi, just go home. I can't, and I won't continue to do this right now. My daughters are upset and scared. My son is screaming, and their mother is in no shape to handle them. I will not leave them like this! Please just go." I stood there frozen in the moment. Shocked, with my heart broken into a million pieces. My husband denied my request for children because he had children with another woman. It was like the world was going in slow motion. I watched in disbelief as my husband consoled his children. I watched as he wiped their tears. I saw the strength of his arms shielding them from the cold reality of the reason behind their existence. They were innocent and clueless. They loved and depended on him. He loved these kids and he had built a family that didn't include me. I watched as my husband closed the door while cradling his two daughters in his arms….two daughters that didn't share my DNA.

I was overcome with rage and I wanted to tear something up. I went to my car and grabbed my knife. I stuck each one of her rimmed up, low profile tires, and then I slashed his on the Benz. I knew that tearing shit up wasn't going to take the pain of what I'd discovered away, but it sure made me feel better for the moment. I jumped in my car and sped away into the night going home alone to face the reality that my marriage really was over, and my life was in fucking shambles.

HERE WE GO AGAIN
(KYRIA WILLIAMS)

A few minutes after making love to JD, Justin started crying. I walked over to the bassinet, picked him up and walked toward the living room. I looked over and noticed that JD was sitting in the foyer with his head in his hands. I walked over to him and asked him if he wanted to hold his son. He looked at me with tears in his eyes, and said, "I would love to hold my boy!"

He was so nervous, and Justin was so tiny compared to his huge hands. I handed him Justin and tried to help steady his shaking hands. Justin opened his eyes and he yawned flashing his cute dimples. JD smiled because he recognized those inherited dimples. He carefully inspected his fingers and toes. He studied his little face and ears. He said, "Wow, he looks like me when I was a baby. I wonder if he has my birthmark." He lifted up his little shirt and noticed that on his stomach just above his bellybutton was a small oval shaped birthmark. It was in the same place as his. "Wow, I can't believe that I have a son! After you left my mother mentioned and old wives' tale, about having dreamt about fish and insisted that I had someone pregnant. I laughed and told her that was not even remotely possible because I was always so careful. Of course, I couldn't tell her about you because she thinks I'm perfect." He winked and flashed a huge grin, and said, "I thought about trying to find you to be certain, but I couldn't bring myself to do it. I didn't want to be that man to cause the breakdown of another mans household. It wasn't until I flew in for a meeting here to discuss business with Malcolm and a mutual friend that my mind changed. It was at that time I saw your picture on his desk and realized that you were his wife and you did in fact have a baby. He talked so much trash about you and I knew at that moment he didn't see you for the priceless gem that you are, so I said fuck it. I knew that I had to try and get to you and the only way to do it was to get closer to Malcolm. I needed to be certain, before I closed the door on you. I wanted to be certain that I didn't miss out on the life of a child, like my father did with me. I always said I was going to be a better father than my father, and this situation does not exempt me from my responsibilities."

He sighed heavily, "Look Kyria, we have to tell him. I can't pretend that this beautiful little boy isn't mine. Why would you want me to?" I looked at him puzzled. He then dropped another bomb saying, "I want you and the baby to come to Miami for a little while. Tell him that you need a break. Look, his greedy ass is going to be working a lot the next few weeks and I think he wouldn't mind or even notice that you are gone. Please sweetheart I need you to do this for me." I thought to myself, this dude is really crazy! How was I supposed to pull this off? I looked into his strong handsome face and could see the sincerity in his eyes. His eyes possessed a childlike innocence. I'd never seen such sincerity in Malcolm's eyes, and having never experienced it, I agreed.

"Ok, we'll come." I immediately felt regret in the pit of my stomach. What was I doing? This was something straight out of the twilight zone. I looked at the clock and realized that it was after 1 and my husband was still not home. I called him to see when he was coming and got no answer. I wanted to allow JD some time with Justin, but I was afraid that Malcolm would come home soon. My phone buzzed, and I looked down, it was a text from Malcolm telling me that he was too drunk to come home, and he had gotten a complimentary room from one of his business associates. I told JD what the text said, and he answered, "Well you see this is the perfect opportunity to leave. Go get packed, we're going to fly out at 6:30."

I hurried upstairs to shower and gathered a few of Justin's essentials. I couldn't believe that I was doing this! JD yelled to me that he was having some things sent to his place from one of the baby boutiques near South Beach. I smiled to myself at his thoughtfulness. I came back and saw that JD had dozed off, and Justin was there lying across his chest, they looked peaceful. The doctors always told Malcolm to hold Justin close to his chest so that he could recognize his heartbeat. They said it helped to calm fussy babies, but he said it was a bunch of foolishness. Apparently, it wasn't, because my fussy infant son was sleeping soundly to the sound of his biological father's heartbeat. My life had turned upside down. My past was now my present and my present was possibly going to become my past.

I walked over to JD and tapped his shoulder, he opened his eyes and said, "What's wrong sweetie?" I said, "Nothing I just wanted to put Justin in his car seat." He kissed Justin's little face and handed him to me. I walked over to his car seat and strapped him in. He was my little angel and he was sleeping peacefully. I returned to the couch where JD was sitting and looked into his beautiful eyes. I told him that I was sorry and that I never meant to hurt him. He grabbed my hands and held them in his and told me that it was ok. He had forgiven me and realized why I did what I did. I told him that every time I looked at Justin I was terrified because he looked nothing like Malcolm. He had every distinct feature of his. I promised him that I would find a way for him to be a part of his son's life. I asked for his patience in dealing with Malcolm. I needed to figure out the way to do this right because one miscalculated step could cause this to go terribly wrong for both of us. Malcolm was ruthless.

He assured me that he understood and leaned in

to kiss me again. I pulled back at first but after a few moments I gave into the magnetic pull of his alluring smile. I kissed him, and chills ran through me as my body's passion seeking cells reactivated with more power than before. My body tingled, and I began to crave for the passion and fury of my lover. I wanted him again, but my body needed him again. We embraced one another once more and fell into the web of lust that we'd woven. Our hips danced their familiar rhythm and we were once again entangled in the passion from before. Every touch and every kiss awakened new desires. They unleashed new power from the core of his body, and my tired, pleasure seeking body was the recipient of his unending love.

I couldn't believe that I was doing it again. I had lost all ability to think concretely and reason. I had fallen hard and became victim to the vulnerabilities of my heart. I was lost in an unfamiliar emotional world and I didn't know if I would ever be able to return.

THE AFTERMATH OF HER VISIT
(MARISSA KINCAID)

I struggled to pull my thoughts and emotions together. I could not believe what I had just heard! Robert walked into the room, and said, "Rissa we need to talk!" I answered angrily, "You're damn right we need to talk Robert, or should I call you Quentin like your wife?" I tried to fight the flood of emotions I was feeling to keep my eyes from being bathed with the sea of tears waiting to overtake them. "I can't believe you've been sleeping with your wife! Is that what you've been doing the last three days?" Robert sat next to me and began to tell me his side. He admitted that he had sex with Chelsi but told me that he woke to find her on top of him and continued to engage.

I didn't know how to feel because technically he could sleep with her if he wanted, she was his wife. I was the one that was out of order by carrying on with a married man. He continued to tell me of his grand revelation about our relationship. He told me that he was taking some time to himself the other day and saw some kids and realized that all of his lies were keeping him from his children and that he had to make things right. He apologized and told me that he could understand if I never wanted to see him again, but he begged me not to take the kids away from him. I didn't know what to say or think. I sat there in disbelief, unable to move or gather my thoughts. I was hurting bad. How could I have been so stupid to expect that this wouldn't blow up in my face. Shame on me.

There was a little knock on the door and it was Arianna. She said, "Mommy....Daddy Brianna is crying, and I can't sleep. She said that you were fighting and that we're not gonna go to live in the big house by the water...Daddy is that true?" She looked up at Robert as those big beautiful eyes of hers were overflowing with tears. He answered, "No Ari, that's not true. Daddy made a mistake and he told some lies and hurt Mommy and another lady. You will still move to the big house by the water, ok sweetie?" She said, "Ok Daddy, but will you come too?" He looked at me and I said, "Yes Ari Daddy will live at the big house by the water with us." I couldn't believe that I fixed my mouth to lie to my baby. I never did that, but I wouldn't be able to stomach seeing her little face filled with the hurt and disappointment of knowing that her Daddy wasn't going to be there.

I hated that I had lied to her. I felt bad. Arianna hugged and kissed me and Robert and skipped into her room. I heard her telling Brianna to stop crying because they were going to live with Daddy in the big house by the water. I went and closed the door behind Arianna. I looked over at Robert and noticed that he had tears streaming down his face. He seemed genuinely remorseful and hurt. He slid closer to me and grabbed my hand. "Rissa, baby, please listen to me. I know that you don't trust me now, but I am asking that you give me the opportunity to prove to you that this is where I want to be. Let me do what I need to do in order to regain your trust. I filed for my divorce and I've decided to give her whatever she wants. I just want to be with my kids. I just want to be with you and build our life together. I know that we started out wrong, but I wish that I'd met you first. Chelsi is not who or what I want anymore. I'm ready to live my life for me."

I looked at him and said, "You don't have to be a father to my kids! Go home to your fucking wife! You slept with her and then came and laid with me! How nasty is that? I trusted that there was nothing physical between you and her. Now you want to talk about doing the right thing for my kids. You didn't give a damn about my kids when you were playing the good husband and laying up with her!" I began to cry, and Robert tried to hold me. I pushed him off of me and screamed, "Don't touch me!" He grabbed me and overpowered me. He held me tightly and continued to plead his case; I stopped fighting and just went limp in his arms. I cried and asked him why? He had no answers and only kept repeating that he was sorry. I cried harder and he kissed me on my face. He began to cry and tears mixed together and we laid there trying to salvage whatever was left.

I drifted off to sleep and in the morning woke to the sound of two wrecker trucks. Apparently in her rage last night, Chelsi had slashed our tires. Robert was standing outside, looking like he was going to collapse at any moment. I walked down the stairs to find the kids dressed and ready to enjoy the day with their Daddy. Brayden was giggling and making baby talk with the girls as they pinched his cheeks and kissed him. Robert walked inside and I shook my head and walked away. He followed me into the kitchen and tried to reason with me once more. He assured me that I'd have my car back in a few hours. I told him that it wasn't about the car; I just wanted the feeling that I had yesterday back. I wanted to trust him.

As much as I wanted to feel sorry for myself I could not help but think of Chelsi and her feelings. What was it like to have your world ripped apart, by learning that your husband had a secret life? I felt like a horrible person, and I really wished that things had been different. I never wanted to hurt another woman; I never sought out to make someone else's husband mine. I just wanted this to go away. Robert stood behind me and held me. I could feel his chest rising and falling. I turned and looked at him. His eyes were red and swollen from the sea of tears he'd cried. He wore the look of a tired, emotionally worn out man. He looked sad and the happy, playful demeanor that he usually had was gone. It was if he was carrying the pain from everyone and it showed clearly on his face.

As much as I wanted to be mad at him, I couldn't help but kiss his lips and tell him that I loved him. I told him that I couldn't promise him anything, but I wanted to try and hold on to whatever we still had left. He told me that he understood and we could move at my pace. He told me that he was going to move me and the kids into the house and he would stay here or in a hotel until I made up my mind if he could stay there. He promised to be there when the girls woke up and when they went to sleep so they would think he was staying there with us. He asked me to be patient and said that he was going to the house to find Chelsi, because he owed her an explanation and he owed her an apology. I watched as he walked into the living room and kissed the kids. He then told them he loved them and that he'd be back soon. I prayed that nothing happened to him. Chelsi was obviously a ticking time bomb, and I couldn't blame her. I would be ready to kill somebody.

HOW DID I END UP HERE?
(CHELSI ADAMS)

I woke up in an unfamiliar hotel suite. My head pounding from the tons of alcohol I'd consumed hours earlier. I laid there in silence and turned my face to realize I wasn't alone. He lay there sleeping beside me peacefully. I closed my eyes and thought, I barely remembered his name. I tried to recall the memories of the hours before. My mind was clouded with erotic images of things that no man, not even my husband had ever done to me. Flashes of him and me in compromising positions continued to invade my mental space. I began to feel my body moisten and become warm from the thoughts of what this strange man and I had done only hours before. He moved and stretched his body, before rolling over. He grabbed me from behind and I could feel his body reliving the moments from before.

He stroked the back of my head and whispered, "This must have been your first time stepping out on your husband?" I answered, "Umm...well... yes it was my first time." He chuckled and said, "Look from what you are telling me this guy was a real jerk to you. I know we are wrong, but I can't just lay here and let these moments go to waste. You see my wife doesn't sleep with me anymore. Who knows when I'll have the pleasure of laying with a woman again. I just want to have you once more and I'll walk away, and you'll walk away, and we'll return to our screwed-up lives. Deal?"

I turned and looked at him and said, "Are you serious? You'd rather sleep with me again than go home to your wife? You are just like my stupid ass husband! I can't do…" I began to raise my voice and before I knew it he was shoving his tongue down my throat again. I tried to fight, but he won. Passion won. He took my love again that morning. He touched me in an animalistic, yet pleasing way and unleashed himself within, with a vengeance. He handled me like a man trying to prove his sexual prowess. I tried to stop myself from falling, but it was so good I couldn't control it.

This stranger that I'd met hours before in the hotel bar was pleasantly violating me. He went full speed ahead and I followed. What was I doing? I didn't know anything about him. I couldn't even remember his name. I wasn't the kind of woman to have a one-night stand, but here I was in the flesh giving myself again to another woman's husband. I thought of the horrible names I called Marissa and realized that I myself was no better than her. At least she was smart enough to get something more out of her infidelity than just a wet ass. We were nearing the end of our time together. I found myself oddly attracted to and intrigued by this dominant, handsome, brown skinned brotha. I didn't usually go for his type, but there was something about him. We rose from the bed, I showered and then he followed. We said our goodbyes and parted ways, planning never to see one another again. I could never allow anyone to know that I had a one-night sex fest with, the brown skinned brotha from the bar.

We exited the hotel at separate times. I looked in my purse for my keys and notice a small piece of paper. It was a handwritten note from him. He had written his cell and office number on there and told me if I ever needed anything to please call him. I think that was an invitation to sleep with him again and not a genuine offer for help. I walked to my car and decided to drive home. I just wanted to shower again, change my clothes, and begin to figure out how I was going to deal with the end of my marriage and Quentin's new family.

I began to think of the things that he said to me. Was it possible that my anger and resentment from him not wanting to have a baby pushed him over the edge? Did I drive him into the arms and the bed of another woman, because of my own selfishness? Did I fail to consider his feelings? I knew that we had problems, but I guess our problems were deeper than I had ever realized. Quentin had never ever cheated on me before. He was always good to me. I realized that my husband was more emotionally fragile than I knew; he needed something that I didn't give him, and unfortunately, he found that in Marissa.

I pulled into the driveway and I noticed a nice car across from the house. I had never seen it before, so I guessed that it was for the neighbor's daughter across the street. It had tinted windows and I was unable to make out the gender of the person in the inside of it. The door opened suddenly at the same time as I was exiting my car. It was Quentin. He looked awful, his clothes were wrinkled, his face and eyes were puffy, and it looked like he had been crying. He seemed to be tired and worn down. I looked at him for a brief moment with empathy, but that soon turned to pure fire fueled rage. I went off! "What the hell do you want, you, pitiful sorry excuse for a man? Why are you here? Go and finish playing house with your little bitch! I have nothing to say to you! You can talk to my lawyer! I'm going to take your sorry ass for everything you're worth and then some. When I'm finished with you, you are going to regret ever cheating! I knew I shouldn't have ever married your trifling ass. I should have gotten back with Jeff…but no, stupid, silly me settled for your pitiful ass."

I stormed into the house and he followed behind me quickly and angrily. I tried to close the door in his face, but he was too strong, and he forced his way into the house.

"Damn it Chelsi!! This is what I am talking about you go off and say horrible shit! Contrary to what you think, I am a MAN and you can't just talk to me like I'm your bitch. You say hurtful, demeaning shit, and purposely try to beat a brotha down emotionally. You run your mouth nonstop! You don't listen, and you play by your own set of rules. You nag, bitch, complain and constantly tear me down, instead of building me up! You never say anything nice or ever show appreciation. You're selfish! I see why your mama is on husband number four! You talk about her but you're just like her! You won't be submissive, are disrespectful and won't shut the fuck up long enough to listen! Do you really think I planned for this to happen? I've never cheated on you in my life; I've never cheated on anyone! I did not mean for this to happen but guess what it did! As much as I wanna wish this fucked up shit away, I can't! I have to look at two women who I've hurt and three kids who I've put in the crossfire of adult bullshit! My heart is broken, because my daughters were afraid that I was leaving them! I never wanted to be a jack in the box daddy to my kids and I have played the role long enough. I jump in and out of their lives like a damned rabbit, and then make up excuses and lies as to why I am not there to tuck them in at night. I leave that girl over there for nights at a time! Alone, tired and hurting. She has no one here but me, yet I ignore her calls and lie to her because I am trying to keep things somewhat civil between you and I. For what though? We don't even talk! We are just like roommates! I do my thing and you do yours. We argue damn near every day! I'm a damned good man who made a huge mistake. A lapse in judgement! I fight these demons and pray every day for sanity because I feel like my mind is slowly being lost in this mess. I came here not to point the finger, but to apologize for not talking to you. I am sorry for not being man enough to talk to you and tell you what happened. I didn't talk to you about what I was feeling and that was wrong. I never gave you the chance to correct your behavior, and for that too, I'm sorry. I let pride and my ego get the best of me and I wasn't honest with you the way I needed to be. Look, I'm not here to fight. I already filed the divorce papers yesterday. I will not contest anything that you ask for. I just want to walk away. You can have all the rental properties, this house, and the other car. I don't want to fight about money because money isn't worth me further devastating my kids; Money isn't worth being a liar or a cheater. I need to be with them. I need to make things right."

I looked at him like he was a damned sci-fi monster, like he had a third eye growing out of his forehead. I thought to myself, this man is crazy, and delusional. I rolled my eyes, and looked straight into his eyes, with a stare of death. "I can't believe you came up in here with that lame excuse and solution! Listen here, stupid ass! Your punk ass better get ready to fight, because like I said when I get done with you, you'll have nothing, and I mean nothing! Now get the hell out of my house before I call the police and tell them you've hit me!" He tried to reason with me, and I walked away.

Irritated, I instinctively grabbed a crystal vase and threw it toward his head. His reflexes were quick, because he ducked just in time to prevent having his head cracked open to the white meat. He looked at me and shook his head saying, "I have flaws and so do you, and your problem is that you fail to recognize and work toward fixing yours...There is no reasoning with you, and you are one crazy bitch! But fuck it, you want a fight; I'll give you a fight. My lawyer will be in touch...I'll be back to get my shit this weekend. Goodbye Chelsi!"

IT'S TIME TO FIGURE THIS OUT
(KYRIA WILLIAMS)

It was nearing 9:30 and JD, Justin and I were well on our way to Miami. I was still in disbelief at what had transpired over the course of the last several hours. My life was headed in a new direction, I didn't know where I was going but I just wanted to continue on the path and see where it was going to lead me. We were flying private and it made things a little more comfortable. JD had absolutely fallen in love with Justin and he held him every chance he got. I normally feed Justin by breast, but I pumped the milk into bottles to allow JD the chance to bond with his son. They had already missed two months. I noticed that JD was very nervous while holding him. He was like a little kid and I had to keep telling him to watch Justin's head. I didn't mind teaching him how to care for a baby, because unlike Malcolm he was interested and eager to learn.

Teaching JD to change a diaper would prove a bit challenging, I tried to warn him, but before I knew it

Justin let it go, and gave the new Daddy a pee shower. He laughed and said, "Hey little man put that thing away!" I told him that he needed to make sure and hurry and cover that little thing up because Justin was a serial peeing machine! I couldn't help but notice that Malcolm hadn't once tried to call me. I guess he was still recovering from his drunken stupor and eventually he'd arrive home and find my note. I told him that I was going to California.

I tried to forget about my uncaring husband, who had left me alone with my infant son as he drank and talked trash to a bunch of stuck up rich folks. I kept glancing over at JD and saw how interested he was in Justin. He played with his little hands and talked to him. Justin managed to smile a few times and display those deep inherited Davis dimples. I could see the joy in JD's face and I was glad that I was able to provide him with such happiness. Justin began to cry, and JD quickly picked him up. He cradled him in his arms and began to rock him. He sang in offkey notes the familiar tune of Hush Little Baby; it was the cutest thing ever. Justin seemed to be easily comforted by JD, I wondered if it was because he could sense that JD was his father. Little Justin dozed peacefully to sleep, and JD put him in his car seat, covered him with a blue satin blanket, and kissed him on his little cheek.

He walked over to me and asked if I was ok. I guess he could see the worry in my face. I was emotionally drained and mentally exhausted. My strawberry blonde, bronze, and chocolate brown, highlighted, mid shoulder length, bone straight hair was pulled into a ponytail. My lashes were gone, my face was puffy, and my eyes were red and irritated from the lack of sleep I had gotten. JD looked tired as well. He had pulled out his laptop and started working; he'd occasionally glance over at me and smile as I curled up in a ball, lounging watching old reruns of Sanford and Son on BET. Even though I knew the way we got to this place was wrong, something about it felt so perfect, it felt so right. It wasn't forced, it came naturally. I never believed in love at first sight and all of that soul mate crap, but my mind was slowly changing, because everything that I wanted in a man was sitting right in front of me in JD.

He was beautiful, educated, a hard worker, attentive, and gracious with his affection. He was considerate, and a gentleman and he seemed to love the idea of being a father, even though he'd only officially known for less than 24 hours. When I lined him up in comparison with Malcolm they were unparalleled.

They were both ambitious and hardworking, they were both providers, but Malcolm lacks one thing that JD has and that is genuine love and compassion. Malcolm is always so cold and hard, sometimes we don't even talk. Not to mention, he and I hadn't been intimate since....well I can't even remember. He doesn't compliment me until I meet his standards. He always wants me to be someone I am not. He is constantly critical of me and always correcting me like a child. I always have to pretend with him, but with JD I can just be Kyria from the block. JD looked over at me and said, "We should be landing in a few. I am going to wrap things up here. I'm sorry I needed to work during this flight. I had a presentation scheduled but I asked if another one of my partners in the firm could take it for me so that I could concentrate on getting you and the baby settled in at the house. I hope you don't mind, but I am having my mother pick us up at the airport."

I was a little shocked, I said, "Oh my God JD you told your mother. She must think I'm a piece of work. I am in no condition to meet her...I look awful." He chuckled and said, "My mother is not judgmental at all she can tell you a few stories about herself. Just relax and be yourself. If I love you that's good enough for my Mama. I'm an only child and a mama's boy, but she knows how to let me handle my own life. She respects my choices as a man and she's not that kind of mother who is overbearing and unbearable." I said ok, but inside I was terrified.

The pilot announced over the intercom that we were close to landing and asked that we fasten our seatbelts and prepare. I looked over at JD as he carefully strapped the airplane seat safety belt across Justin's car seat. He looked up at me and smiled and said, "Well, are you ready to meet my Mama?" I chuckled and shook my head no. We laughed and exchanged sweet smiles to one another. He blew a kiss at me and I placed my hand out and motioned as if I was grabbing it and holding it in my hand. I sat there still trying to digest it all. I couldn't believe that I was there with him. The plane landed, and it began to taxi down the runway to the private hanger portion of the airport. I looked out the window and was excited to be there and ready to embrace the sunshine and sand. I was ready to dance in the ocean. The plane came to a stop and the pilot came and told us that it was okay to exit. The door was opened, and we walked toward the black Range Rover waiting on standby near the runway. As we got closer, a small framed, woman with short blonde hair quickly approached us.

She was a beautiful woman, who was quite fashionable. She was wearing a sundress and a fierce pair of wedged sandals covered with earth toned rhinestones. She waved at JD and was smiling hard. She began to move a little faster and before you know it she was in JD's arms. He hugged her and kissed her and said, "Mama! I missed you! He lifted her in the air and she said, "Oh my Jayson! Boy I missed you too! Now put me down and let me take a look at that baby!" She walked over to me and said, "Oh lord, look at this little man here! He looks like you Jay! He is so beautiful!" She leaned over and took Justin out of his seat and began to kiss his little face. JD smiled and said, "Mama, this is Kyria, Justin's mother."

She smiled at me and handed Justin to JD and

gave me a big hug. She said, "Oh, hello sweetie! I'm
Adella, Jayson's mother. You are such a beautiful
girl! I am so pleased to meet you. Thank you for
coming here for me to meet my grandson. I know
this is hard for you honey, but please know that I am
so happy and thankful to have you here." I smiled
back and said, "Thank you so much. I am glad that
we came, and I am glad that you are happy!" She
said, "Now Jayson, give me back my grandson. I
need to give him some more kisses."

JD loaded the bags into the truck, and strapped
Justin's car seat in. He hopped in the driver seat and
asked me to sit in the passenger side, because he
knew his mama wanted to be in the back seat with
Justin. We drove from the airport and went to a nice
gated community a few miles from the beach. We
pulled into the driveway of a nice cottage style home,
with beautiful landscaping. The grass was perfectly
manicured, and I fell in love with the pretty wrought
iron fence that surrounded the house. There were
rows and rows of huge, gorgeous palm trees. We
walked into the house and it was elegant, yet cozy. It
had vaulted ceilings and a spacious foyer. It was
amazing.

It had an open floor plan and its furnishings were
African art themed. I looked around and noticed the
beautiful plants that lined the huge bay window in
the living room. Adella lead me to where I could get
myself and Justin settled in. She led me down the
hall to a beautiful guest suite that was equipped with

a personal bathroom. She told me to make myself comfortable, and that there was an adjoining sitting room and it had everything I needed for both me and Justin. In the room was a beautiful mahogany crib, with Winnie the Pooh bedding. It was perfect. I was so impressed by JD and his mother's thoughtfulness. I told eager and ecstatic new Grandmother that I needed to nurse Justin and that as soon as I was done, I'd be happy to give him to her. She smiled and said ok and left the room. I sat in the beautiful rocking chair that was in the room and held Justin close to me;

There was a knock at the door and then JD peeked in and asked if it was ok for him to come in. I said "Sure, you can." He said, "I don't want you to be mad at me or uncomfortable." I said, "Ummmmmmmm, it's a little too late for that. You told your Mother about our situation?" He smiled and said, "Yes, I tell my Mother everything. She won't judge. Trust me she's not like that at all. She is the most understanding person I have ever met." He reached out and grabbed my hand and told me not to worry. I tried not to obsess over what I believed that Adella thought of me. I smiled and squeezed his hand. He kissed my hand and winked.

I thought to myself I must be dreaming this is too good to be true. He slid close to me and reached over and started rubbing Justin's head. He looked up and said, "I know that being here is difficult for you, but my Mother is elated. I'm her only child; Justin is her only grandchild. That is until you marry me, and we have our daughter." I chuckled at him and said, "Ok, whatever Jayson...you play too much!" He smiled and said, "No I don't play too much, you'll see, I'm not into games." He kissed me on my forehead and told me when he'd have his mama to come and pick up Justin while I showered and got changed. He said he was leaving for a while he had some business to take care of. I sat there still trying to understand where my life was going, so many things had changed.

A few moments later I was burping Justin and there was a knock on the door. It was Adella. She walked in with a great big smile on her face and said, "Jayson told me that you wanted to get bathed and changed." I nodded and said, "Yes, I feel so tense and a nice bath and a change of clothes will do wonders." I handed her Justin and I admired how she just seemed to love all over him. She was so careful with him and seemed to have a special touch. She walked out of the room and told me take my time and to even take a nap and rest if I wanted to. She assured me that Justin was okay, and I thanked her for everything. I walked into the bathroom of the guest suite and began to run my bath water. I wondered why I hadn't heard anything from Malcolm. Surely, he knew we were gone by now. But then again, he probably didn't care. I ran back into the room to grab my cell phone in case there were any calls. I checked it several times to make sure I hadn't missed anything. As I scrolled through the call log I noticed that there was not one call from my husband, could it be that he really didn't care? I turned off the water and stepped into the big garden tub. I found myself sinking and so relaxed as I peered out of the window and embraced the beautiful scenery of the private courtyard outside. I felt myself drifting into a place of peace, a place that I had not seen in such a long time.

For the first time I was actually relieved to be away from Malcolm and all of his foolishness. I continued to relax and then out of the blue my phone rang. I grabbed and looked at the caller ID and it was Malcolm. I answered, "Hello..." He screamed, "Where in the fuck are you Kyria? I've been trying to call you! I don't know what you are trying to pull by disappearing, but you need to get back here right mutha-fuckin now! You don't leave without my permission! I can't believe your ungrateful ass decided to leave all because you were mad at me for handling business! All that business I handled last night is what keeps you dressed in all those nice clothes and driving good and living good. You need to get your ass back here to Indianapolis or you are going to find yourself back in the projects where I found you...Kyria do you understand me?"

I sat there listening to this man who claimed to love me talk to me like I was a child. He belittled and insulted me. He talked down to me every chance he got. It seemed like every time I didn't do what he wanted, he continually threw my past back up in my face. He had no problem reminding me that I lived a different life before meeting him. He made it no secret that he felt that he was better than me because he had wealth and social status.

What was I going to do? There was no way that I could stay gone and subject myself to the abuse that was going to result from me being away from Malcolm. I didn't want to hear him talk to me like a dog, but how was I going to get away from him?

Malcolm was ruthless and was not above putting his hands on me. He'd done it before. Knowing him he'd probably track my phone and send someone to find me. He certainly has enough money to do so. I didn't know what I was going to do. Nothing was set in stone and guaranteed with me and JD, but I knew that he genuinely cared and loved me. The one thing I was certain of is that I had to go back to Indianapolis at some point soon and face Malcolm. I just didn't know when. I just had to go.

SHOULD I STAY, OR SHOULD I GO
(MARISSA KINKAID)

It had been a few hours since Robert left the house. I was still a little shocked by the events that had transpired hours before. I tried to remain calm because the girls were watching me. Brayden was asleep in his swing and the girls were lying in the floor watching their favorite show, "Dora The Explorer." I attempted to not be consumed with thoughts about what was going on at Robert's house. I really didn't know what to think or to believe anymore. He seemed as if he was remorseful and really wanted to do right, but could I really compete with the history that he and Chelsi shared? Could we really have something great from this situation? I tried to think of something else but the images of events that happened the evening prior kept replaying in my mind like a horrible video rerun.

I paced the living room floor and eventually went into the kitchen to start cooking dinner. I guess part of me really wanted Robert to come home to me and his kids, but I couldn't help but feel ashamed and extremely foolish because of the situation. I began to cook dinner and then I heard the girls yell excitedly, "Daddy!!!! Daddy!!!! You're back!" I smiled a little on the inside because I really wanted to have him here with us again.

Robert walked into the kitchen and he didn't say anything. I tried to ask him what happened, but he quickly covered my mouth with his hand and grabbed me and held me tightly. He told me that he loved me and begged me to please forgive him for complicating my life in such a way. He apologized for his lies and promised that he'd always be straight with me. I pulled away from him and told him that I loved him, but I didn't know if I'd ever be able to trust him, and that I wasn't certain that our relationship could last. I didn't know if I could take the drama that was coming, and I didn't want to subject my kids to anymore of the foolishness that we both caused.

He told me to please reconsider and not to make any hasty decisions. He said that he was going to prove to me that he loved me and the kids and wanted to be a family. I turned and continued to prepare my dinner, but inside my heart I knew that letting Robert go was something that I wasn't going to be able to do easily. My mouth said one thing but my heart sang a totally different song.

After preparing dinner, the kids, Robert and I sat down to eat. I couldn't help but smile as the girls tried to out talk one another to fight for Robert's attention. Arianna kept telling him about the frog growing story that she heard on the Discovery Kids channel and Brianna kept telling him about the dog who walked on two legs. He sat there and gave them his undivided attention and as funny as their stories were, he sat there listening intensely with a straight face. He had the perfect daddy touch. The girls finished their dinner and I told them to go upstairs and get ready for their baths. Robert told me that he'd clean up the kitchen and that I needed to rest while I could; he assured me that he'd take care of everything. I went upstairs and stretched my sluggish body across the bed. I guess my body was more tired than I had imagined. I laid there and in an instant, I was out cold.

After a few hours of deep sleep, I woke to find myself in total darkness, still clothed and covered with a throw blanket. I got up and peeked in on the girls and they were sleeping soundly. Brayden was in my room in his crib knocked out too. I walked downstairs and saw that Robert was sitting there watching TV. He looked up and saw me coming down and asked me to join him on the couch. I went over, and he looked into my eyes and told me that he loved me. I tried to resist the urge to kiss his lips, but it proved too much for me. So, there we were locked and engaged in a passionate kiss. It felt so good to kiss him, it felt so right. He slowly began to caress my neck and shoulders and before you know it his hands were exploring every part of my body. I wanted him to love me that night. I wanted him to hold me in his arms and never let me go. I stopped and looked into his eyes and said, "Robert, please don't play with my heart. Don't sell me dreams and play these mind games…If you can't be real with me please just let me go. Things have gotten out of hand and you really need to make a decision. There will be no more back and forth. I have to know that things are over for you and her!" He smiled and said. "Baby I promise, I'm not playing with you. I want you, I need you…I love you. This is not anything I'd wish on my worst enemy. I'm ashamed and know that this is my fault. Please trust me and allow me to fix."

He continued his quest to gain control of my body. His hands moved over every inch my skin; I felt his warm breath on the back of my neck as he kissed me from there to the middle of my back. I lost it all and again I was stuck in the whirlwind of emotions. He traveled to the depths of my love again. He held me close and pushed and pushed until finally he had reached the goldmine within me. My body was a ship and its crew had committed mutiny against me. He was the new captain and he conquered every area of the secret spaces within me. His manhood journeyed to places far and with every moment he covered more and more ground. I felt as if I was going to go mad, out of my mind and my body was unable to fight off the side effects from the passion that my lover was giving me. With him exploring me from the inside out, I began to quiver, and my body was unable to hold back the eruption that was now bursting forth from within me.

Suddenly Robert's body stiffened and tensed and there we were together dancing in the parade of orgasmic bliss…feeling each other from the inside out, reigniting the love that was recently injured and threatened, the love that started from a conversation, the love that had brought pain to another, the love that was forbidden and scoffed at by the world, the love that yielded three beautiful and innocent children, the love that I never wanted to end.

It was as if we were falling once more. The feeling he and I shared in that moment was all that mattered. I wanted his body to keep pleasuring mine; I wanted him to launch himself deeper and deeper until he reached a place that gave him everything that he needed to feel how much I loved him. I wanted him to know how much I wanted him in my life; I wanted him to know how much I needed him in my life. After hours of dancing our lovemaking dance its end was upon us. I could feel Robert's manhood pulsate within the confined space of my body as he released all of his erotic energy into me. He kissed me tenderly and there we were once again. Bodies twisted and tangled in the sea of one another. We were quietly suspended in the sweet feeling of one another's arms.

So, there I lay with my lover beside me sleeping peacefully and uninterrupted. I tried to trick my mind into sleeping but was unsuccessful in doing so. There I was with my eyes fixed on the ceiling thinking....my mind racing. I couldn't help but think of Chelsi. I wondered if she was thinking of us and somewhere plotting her next move of revenge. I didn't want to seem as if I could care less about her feelings, but one part of me, the selfish part was only concerned about me and mine. I never thought that I would ever find myself in such a predicament, how did this happen? I know that those who are sympathetic to my plight are far and few in between. In the court of relationships, I know I'm already tried and convicted of "1st degree home-wrecking".

In situations such as mine, no one ever stops to look at the side of the other woman; they are only concerned with the feelings of the main woman. The truth of the matter is that I have never cheated with or even looked at another woman's man, let alone her husband. Me and Robert just happened, and every day I live with the fact that I made a mistake by getting involved with him. I have many regrets, but life can't be lived based on regrets. I don't regret my children. I am concerned about everyone involved in this situation, but I am the most concerned about those three innocent children who are now caught in the barrage of adult foolishness. I must protect my kids from the truth of how they came into this world. I could never allow them to know they were conceived as a result of two weak adults. I could never let them know that Mommy was once the chick on the bench and not the starter. In their little minds we are a family, and I wouldn't allow anyone to take that away from them. I love my kids and could never live with myself if the truth was exposed. A person's perception is their reality even if that reality is false, and my babies' reality is very false. It's more false and fucked up than their little minds have the power to process.

Hours passed and sleep wasn't an option for me, I decided that I was going to hop in the shower and go down and fix breakfast for Robert and the kids. I needed to move fast because I'm sure that Brayden would be waking soon for a diaper change and a bottle. I ran into the bathroom and hopped into the shower. I hit the places that counted and hurried to get out and dry myself. I went back into the bedroom and Brayden was lying across Robert's chest, he must have awoken while I showered, and Robert put him back to sleep. They laid there looking like twins, mouth wide open, slobbering, snoring and all. I slipped on a pair of charcoal grey sweats and a white t-shirt. I pulled my hair back in a ponytail and walked out of the room closing the door quietly behind me.

When I got downstairs I noticed that my phone had a missed call. It was a private call. I pressed the voicemail icon and began to listen to the message. It was Chelsi, she sounded like she was beyond wasted. She told me to watch my back and that I needed to know that she was after me and that she was going to make sure me and Robert both paid big time. I sat there and felt tears began to well up in my eyes because I was frustrated and pissed at myself. This was too much drama for me and I know that my daddy was turning over in his grave. I didn't know what was going to happen next, but I knew that things were going to get much worse before they got any better. I knew that eventually I was going to be paid a visit from the all-knowing and relentless bitch named Karma.

I knew that Chelsi was going to do everything to make sure I hurt as much as she did, and truthfully, I really couldn't blame her. Chances are I'd probably be the same way. Most women would be the same way. I couldn't imagine her pain. Mine was definitely nothing in comparison to hers. I didn't know much about Chelsi, but I recall Robert saying that she was very sweet, but ruthless when it came to getting what she wanted. I didn't know much but the one thing I could be certain of is that Chelsi wasn't going to bow out gracefully and I was going to be in the fight of my life because hell hath no fury like a woman scorned and Chelsi was the epitome of a woman scorned.

RETURNING THE FAVOR
(CHELSI ADAMS)

After leaving a threatening message on the tramp's voicemail, I stumbled my drunk ass into the living room and continued to drink on my third full bottle of Moscato. I just wanted to get sloppy drunk and forget about the fact that my entire life was in shambles. I still had love for my husband even though we were unrepairable, and things were over.

I was a little lonely and I decided that I'd use the number that was in my purse. I couldn't believe that I called him to come and visit me. I knew that he only wanted me for sex but at this time in my life, any attention was good attention.

Hell, my husband was laying up playing house, so why couldn't I do the same? The hateful part of me wanted another wife to feel the pain that I was feeling. I heard the doorbell ring and it was Malcolm he walked into the house and said that I looked like crap. Who the hell was this fool talking to? He asked me if it was cool to be in the house considering that my husband had a key. I told him that I didn't care, and it didn't matter because he had no control over anything that I did anymore.

We sat there for a few minutes and Malcolm asked me if I wanted to go stay at his place to get away. I was so drunk I told him yes and he scooped me up and put me in his car. I couldn't remember anything after that but finding myself naked in his bedroom. I knew that being there was so wrong because two wrongs didn't make a right, but I needed to feel better about my situation and if laying with this man was going to do it then, I was all for it.

Malcolm walked into the room and I studied his body. I guess I didn't realize how big he was. He wasn't chubby, but he was just stocky. He walked over to me and asked me if I was sure that I wanted to go there again. I told him yes and he popped a couple of pills, took a sip of water and after a few moments I found myself once again in a compromising position with another woman's husband.

Right then and there, I didn't care about anything; Malcolm was the fix I needed. His strong hands and soft lips found their way to every crease and fold of my skin. He didn't miss a spot. I had never felt such intensity from any man before. It was as if we both were releasing anger and energy into one another. He went after me relentlessly, nonstop. I tried to catch my breath, but it seemed as if every minute with him took away everything that I had. In my heart I knew this was wrong but, in my head, I had justified my behavior and I didn't want this man to stop. I took his power and strength and packed it neatly away within me.

I scrambled and hurried myself from one plateau to the next. I was losing the battle and he was winning. I had to flip the script. I regrouped and was ready to return the favor. We tossed and turned until I was in the place of dominance. He was then under my control and subject to my rules. I gave him every ounce of hated and rage I felt. I was angry and clawed and carved my mark into him to make sure that she would be aware that I had been there.

We were into the homestretch of our indiscretion and the animalistic sound of his baritone voice echoed out in the room as I felt his body roaring within like a lion commanding his loyal jungle subjects. He was there, and I was there too, we bellowed out screams as both of our bodies reacted in sync to the pleasure being given from the other. After the exchange of passion and power we both lay there drained and exhausted. All I wanted to do was sleep and hope that I would wake up from a bad dream. My head was spinning, and I was nauseous from the liters of wine that I consumed. I guess you could say that during the course of 48 hrs., I'd become a love toy to a married man and a drunk all at once. What a fucking life!

As I began to sober up, I couldn't believe that I had done this. What the hell was I doing with myself? I was so out of control, and truthfully, I was no better than Quentin or Marissa. I was better than this. It was clear that I was nothing to this man, and how had I stooped so low as to give myself away freely without commitment and demands? I didn't know this man from Adam, but here I was once again laid up in his arms, body weak and sore from biological warfare. Drunken passion and pleasure were the only things that were on my mind. My moral compass was broken, and badly misdirected. I wanted to get up and go, but I couldn't. I wouldn't. I needed to feel better and if this was what it took, then so be it. So, there I was again soliciting a reaction from the brown skinned professional brotha that I'd only met 24 hrs. earlier.

I manipulated my body to once again become a part of his and again found myself in another moment of indiscretion with another woman's husband, while my husband laid his head on a pillow and shared a bed with some other woman. After adventuring into the world of passion once more with Malcolm I finally found myself able to sleep without caring what happened next. Our deed was done, and we could return to reality the next day. I didn't care who I hurt at that moment. My mind was a mess and stuck on revenge. The only person I cared about was myself. I got what I needed and got what I wanted. Fuck it.....life goes on.

Malcolm and I lay there together in his huge master suite. I drifted in and out of sleep still being affected by the alcohol that I consumed all alone. My head felt like it was going to explode at any moment. It was the most horrible feeling that I had ever felt. I closed my eyes again tightly and hoped that the pain would go away, but to my surprise the pain was going to get worse. I found myself in such an uncaring mode. I found myself conflicted yet trying to continually find justification for my actions. Malcolm lay there peaceful with his strong arms tightly wrapped around me. I tried to resist the feeling of guilt that was beating deeply within my soul. I needed to regain some sense of dignity. How was it that my life was such a mess? Who had I become? I didn't care to give consideration to the fact that we were both married and no matter the condition of the relationship those vows weren't to be taken lightly. We both had stood before God, our family, and friends declaring our love for our life partners. I tried to steady the thoughts that were in my mind because I wanted to make sense of what was really going on in my life. My life was in a rapid downward spiral, and for the most part I didn't know whether I was coming or going.

HE'S PLAYING FOR KEEPS
(KYRIA WILLIAMS)

After the disturbing call that I had gotten from Malcolm, I finished getting myself together. I decided that the only way I was going to be able to have any peace was to return home and deal with
    Malcolm face to face. I didn't know how I was going to break the news to him, but I had to do it. I continued to put on my clothes trying to stop focusing on dealing with the situation so that I could enjoy Miami and all of its beauty. I walked into the bedroom and on the bed was a garment bag with a note attached. It was from JD.

My Dearest Kyria,
I know that things have been crazy the last day or so. I want to make sure that you have the opportunity to enjoy a little bit of the beauty that Florida has to offer. I have made arrangements for Momma to keep the baby because I want to spend a little time with you. I know that you are going through a lot emotionally right now, but I hope that you will allow me the pleasure of

taking you out and showing you a good time. I took the liberty of ordering you some items that I think that you would like. I hope that you like them, so just get dressed and meet me outside when you are done. I will be there waiting for you. -JD

I unzipped the garment bag to find the most beautiful sundress I'd ever seen. It was the color of the beautiful aquamarine water that you see in the pictures from the Caribbean. It was a halter and the top of it was covered with the most beautiful colors. I looked at the floor and saw that there were the most beautiful sandals to match. I couldn't believe that this man had done this for me. Even though I knew that I needed to deal with my situation, the idea of a night out in the beautiful city of Miami was more appealing to me at the moment. I felt as if it was what I needed to escape from the reality of what was happening in my life. So I got dressed and made sure that I put my makeup on perfectly to match the beautiful outfit that JD had purchased for me. I didn't know what to do with my hair because it was such a mess, so I decided to pull it back into a simple ponytail. I slipped on my shoes, dabbed a little of my favorite fragrance on my wrists, neck and behind my ears. I was all set to spend some much needed time with him. I walked out of the front door and was looking for JD; I didn't see his car and wondered where he was. I looked up and there he was walking toward me from across the lawn. He looked so good. He had on a nice two piece white linen short set and some nice brown leather sandals. He had a fresh cut and neatly trimmed mustache and goatee. He was like something out of a dream. He left the top three buttons of his shirt open and I could see his beautiful muscular chest peeking out from the little opening. I stood there in awe of this beautiful man that was coming my way. I wanted someone to pinch me or slap me or something because I still thought I was dreaming. He walked up to me and grabbed my hand and said, "You look beautiful...thank you for accepting my offer, I promise you that you won't be disappointed."

We walked out of the gate and we walked to his Silver Convertible Mercedes. It was stunning! He opened the car door for me and I got in. My heart was beating fast and I started to feel butterflies within the pit of my stomach. I tried to not be nervous, but it was like I was a schoolgirl going on her first date. JD was wonderful and being with him seemed to make everything much better. I felt safe and secure with him. I felt wanted, loved and needed. He had a way of making me feel like I was the one and only woman in the entire world.....the one and only woman who mattered in his world. This was such a change from the norm.

Malcolm and I didn't do anything like this anymore. In the beginning he wined and dined me. It's almost like he did what he had to do to get me and when I married him everything stopped. He turned cold and heartless…well actually he was always cold and heartless, but I was just blinded and fooled by the money. I admired JD because he was the perfect gentleman and I could tell that he was trying to do everything to make sure that I knew how much he cared for and wanted to be with me. I realized that I actually could fall in love with him.

Here I was in this amazing place with a beautiful man. I was with a man that clearly loved and cherished me more than the man who I had exchanged vows with. From the moment I met JD he was nothing but a perfect, it was like he knew just how to treat a woman. He knew what to say and what to do to make a woman feel like a queen. He asked me if I was ready for a road trip, I smiled and asked, "Where are we going?" He said, "We're going to experience the beauty of Key West." I smiled once more and sat back and enjoyed the ride. Our drive was a little over three hours and I enjoyed it. We listened to the smooth R&B sounds as we drove and enjoyed one another's company. JD would occasionally look over at me and ask if I was ok. I'd nod yes, and he'd smile and continue to concentrate on the road. Finally, after our nice little adventure on the road we arrived in Key West. The place was beautiful. We arrived at our destination, it was a beautiful resort. We walked in the building and there was a small framed gentleman waiting for us. "Hello, Mr. Davis I'm glad you've arrived we have been waiting for you. Please you and the lady follow us this way." We followed the man and he led us to this beautiful suite, it was more like a little apartment. It had everything we needed to be comfortable. I was blown away and ready to share this amazing time with JD. We went to dinner, had a few drinks, we walked the streets and then we ended our night by visiting the Southernmost point of the US. It was amazing to see that we were only 90 miles away from Cuba. We sat there staring out at the water, glaring at the beautiful stars.

I noticed how the water was still an uninterrupted looking like a huge mirror reflecting the contents of the darkened but crisp and clear night sky....It was beautiful, and it reminded me of the first time JD and I had spent time together. This time was different because his role had changed...he wasn't just a fling but the father of my child. I was falling in love with JD. Everything about him was what I wanted and needed. I didn't know how I was going to keep him in my life but I was going to. I couldn't and wouldn't return to the misery of a loveless, material driven relationship with my judgmental and uncaring husband. I was going to have a family for my son and it was going to be with JD.

We finished our trip to the Southernmost point by writing our names on a huge boulder that had been signed by countless other visitors...it was fun, and I would never forget the time that we spent there. We headed back to the resort, and I called to check in on Justin. Adella said that he was sleeping peacefully and had just had a fresh bottle and diaper change. She assured me that he was ok and told me to please try and have a good time. After my call, I sat there looking at JD and tried to make sense of everything. It was still as if I was dreaming and in the twilight zone. I didn't want to bring drama into anyone's life and I knew that this was going to be some serious drama for JD. I didn't tell him that I had spoken to Malcolm and that he demanded that I return home immediately. I saw that he was so happy and enjoying our time together and I really didn't want to take that away from him. The truth of the matter is that Justin and I had to return to Indianapolis soon, because if we didn't there was going to be some major problems. Malcolm was cold, calculating and ruthless and he'd find a way to locate me. Besides I knew that JD had to return to Indianapolis himself to continue to work on the business with Malcolm also.

JD must have noticed that I was worried, so he asked me what was wrong, and I said, "Nothing, I'm just in awe of everything that has happened. I never would have imagined a year ago that I would see you, or even be here with you again. I thought that I would have to take the secret of my child to my grave, but here we are." He said, "Yes sweetheart here we are….here we are together, and hopefully soon it will be this way forever." He opened his arms and I instantly fell into them. He held me close and told me that everything would be alright. There I was again feeling complete happiness, with this perfect man, in this perfect place trying to forget that I had to return to the reality of my life and face my problems head on.

At that moment I didn't want to have to do anything but continue to feel the love that was radiating from the heart of this man whom I shared a child with...the man who I wanted to eventually share my life with. JD then whispered in my ear that he loved me, and I couldn't deny what I was feeling, and I looked into his beautiful captivating eyes and responded, saying that I loved him too. In that very instant it felt as if my heart was complete. How could it be that I loved this man in such a way? Could it be that I was really in love with him this entire time but because of the fear of losing everything, I suppressed it, tucked it away discreetly, away from the surface? I just wanted the feeling to last. I wanted my heart to remain full.

Upon the heels of my confession of love, the passion was reignited, and JD and I began to love one another in our own special way. His touch, his kiss, and his strong embrace incarcerated me, and I was once more a prisoner of his love. I was overwhelmed by the feeling that he was giving me. It was if my body was under his total control, and that was quite ok with me. It felt as if we were supposed to be there together, loving and exploring one another again.

We were both overtaken by the affection from the one another and our bodies reacted accordingly. I found myself lost in the motion and feeling of his body tangled within me. With each second of time our bodies continued toward the peak of complete satisfaction. We lay there together, holding one another closely, kissing, touching…while our bodies moved perfectly in tandem. I felt the force from JD nearing the climax of his quest for satisfaction. He held me tighter, he pushed harder, he propelled himself deeper until he was unable to contain the release of everything he had…he'd given me his total self and I had given him all of me.

My mind was going a thousand miles a minute because I knew that this had to end…I knew that I had to bring myself back to reality, but even though that was in the forefront of my mind I buried it and concentrated on the wonderful man that rested his exhausted body within my arms.

I kissed him and played with the waves in his hair, wishing to hold on to this piece of time forever. I tried to forget for that moment that there was more that needed to be done. I knew that before I could fully walk through this door, I needed to close the other door that was open wide and full of conflict and scandal in Indianapolis. JD rolled onto his back and motioned for me to lay my head on his chest. I slid myself over and laid my head on his chest and was lulled into a peaceful slumber by the unique song that his heart sang…a song of love…a song that I needed and wanted to hear forever...a song that I wasn't going to lose, regardless of what it cost me.

WHERE DO WE GO FROM HERE?
(MARISSA KINCAID)

Breakfast was done, and I hurried up the stairs to wake the kids and Robert. I wanted to make sure that none of them overslept and were able to enjoy the feast that I had created for us all. I walked upstairs and noticed that the kids were already up, they were sitting in their room in the middle of the floor with Robert and Brayden watching their favorite Saturday morning Nick Jr. cartoon lineup. I smiled because they seemed to really love being with their father. Robert looked up and saw me standing there and said, "Hey Baby, Good Morning!" I smiled and told him that breakfast was ready and that he and the kids needed to come down and eat. I walked away from the room and suddenly my heart sank because I realized that I was living in a fantasy world. Here I was playing house with this man, who lawfully was bound to another woman. I struggled but managed to dismiss the thoughts that were plaguing my mind and continued to prepare to have breakfast with my "family".

The girls and Robert had their breakfast and I tried to stop my mind from going into guilt mode. I watched the happiness in the eyes of my children as they enjoyed the time that they were spending with their father. It was unhurried and uninterrupted, and that was something that they weren't used to. Arianna and Brianna both were beaming as Robert crawled around on all fours acting like a horse while they held on to his neck screaming "giddy-up Daddy...giddy-up". Brayden scooted his little body across the floor after them trying to keep up with Robert and the girls as they played joyfully on the floor of the family room.

The room was filled with boisterous sounds of happiness that could and would only come from children playing and enjoying time with their father. This was everything that I had ever wanted, but I was terrified that it soon would come to an end. My heart was sinking more and more as I tried to embrace the truth of my situation. Regardless of the fact that Robert was here now, he had to return to his life and deal with the impending facts of his divorce. A divorce that was in fact, going to be a nasty one. Chelsi was out for blood and if she had it her way Robert was going to pay with more than just his money, he was going to pay emotionally.

After their much-needed fun session with their father the girls were ready to get their clothes on and prepare for the day that Robert had promised them. He promised them that he would take them to Dave

& Busters and the movies. They were so excited and raced to get themselves ready for their much-anticipated Daddy and Daughters day out. Brayden was a little exhausted from playing also; he laid his little head down on Robert's chest as they both relaxed in the middle of the floor. I picked him up and put him in his playpen. Robert looked at me and I guess he could see the turmoil in my face, he asked me what was wrong, and I just lost it and broke down crying hysterically. He walked over to me and grabbed my hand and tried to console me while investigating the reason for my unexpected loss of emotional control.

My face was flooded with tears, and I couldn't help it I had to tell him what I was feeling. I had to tell him the truth about my fears. We sat there on the couch and I began to tell my lover of the plethora of emotions that I was experiencing. "Robert, baby I must be honest with you, this isn't easy for me because I feel like things are really up in the air with us. I know you say that we are going to be together as a family, but I must admit that I am so scared that you will not follow through with the plan. I am terrified that you are going to leave me and the kids because you are still in love with your wife. After all you did just sleep with her! I know you want me to trust you, but how can I really trust you and you did this to her? What makes me exempt? You and her have more history than you and I and why would you be faithful to me and not to her? I can't compete with your history and I don't know if

I am strong enough to handle the battle that is going to result from you filing for divorce. I love you, but I love myself more! I must protect myself and my kids, and I refuse to let you or anyone else hurt them. So, I suggest that you keep it moving if you are playing games with my heart. This is the real deal and I refuse to let you sell me another dream, don't talk about it Robert! Be about it!"

He stood there looking at me puzzled as if I was speaking some sort of foreign language. Brayden began to whimper a little in his sleep. Robert shook his head and walked over to Brayden's playpen to pick him up. He turned and looked at me with the same puzzled look on his face and said, "Look Marissa, I don't know if you have realized it or not, but my life is in pure chaos right now! My wife just found out that I have not one, not two, but three children with another woman. I don't know if you think that this is easy for me, but I am responsible for causing more pain than I have ever experienced in my life. This is not a game to me, this is not just something to do....you and my kids are not just something to do. I'm tired of playing the double role, and God knows I'm tired of living a lie. I want a normal life, a normal relationship, one that is free from sneaking and scheming. I am tired of lying to my kids about where I am at night....I'm tired of missing my kids and missing moments. I am tired of being less than honorable as a man and a father, and I am trying to make things right. Look I can't do anything about what is already been done and I refuse to be backed into a corner like I am the only person who is at fault here. I didn't put a gun to your head and force you to be with me! You decided that you were in just like I did and guess what we have to both face the reality of what is going to happen because of our choices! So please don't get all self fucking righteous and play the damned victim! I'm not going to be a coward any longer and hide behind excuses. I am going to be a real man and face the music, and deal with whatever consequences I have to deal with because of my actions. I can't amend for anything that has been done. You've been hurt, Chelsi's been hurt, and my kids have been hurt. The only thing I can do is to ask God to forgive me and pray that Chelsi forgives me too and make a choice to move on. I want to be here with you Marissa, here with you and my kids, but I am not going to be held captive by your insecurities! I'm not going to try to prove myself over and over again! I'm not going to jump through hoops to appease your ass. I've said a lot and now it's time to let my words and my actions match period! So, if you decide you don't want me, then please do me a favor and let me know and I'll just be a father to my kids and nothing to you. Because at the end of the day the only people that matter most to me are Arianna, Brianna, and Brayden! Now you take that how you want it! I have nothing else to say about it! Now I need to get my girls and give them a fun day as I promised. Let me know what you decide….I'm gone!"

He was pissed, and I knew it. He stormed out of the room and called for the girls to come and get ready to leave. I looked at him and could not believe that he had taken such a tone with me. He got the kids ready, told them to kiss me goodbye and then they walked out of the door. I was left standing there alone. I looked out the window and watched as Robert drove away. I slumped down into the lounge chair and the tears seemed to flow with much more intensity.

What was I going to do? What was I going to say to him? Was I going to walk away from him and just become another single unwed mother? Was I going to try and fight for this love that I felt so deeply inside for this man with whom I shared three beautiful children? I really wished that I could just forget about everything, but I knew I had to deal with this. It needed to be settled. I had to make a decision, and this decision would ultimately not only change my life, but it would change the lives of my innocent children. If I made the wrong decision there were definitely going to be some casualties, and who those casualties would be was totally dependent on what I chose to do....the ball was in my court, and the play book was in my hand. I needed to act fast because the play clock was running out quickly.

BACK TO REALITY
(CHELSI ADAMS)

After my latest drunken encounter, I returned to the comfort of home trying to regroup and regain some sense of control. I got in and walked into the living room. I was overtaken with emotion when I looked at all of the pictures that were lining the mantle of my fireplace. I never imagined that my marriage would ever be like this. I had heard of horror stories from the marriages of others, but to find myself in such a situation was surreal.

I noticed that I had voicemails, so I picked up the phone and checked the messages. There were three, one from my son, and two from my lawyer. I listened to the message from my son Alex; it was great to hear his voice. He was so excited because he had gotten straight A's and made the high honor roll in school. He reminded me that I promised to get him an I-Pad if he got straight A's, so he was calling to make sure that I kept my end of the bargain. I laughed to myself because that kid was hilarious; he was definitely his mother's child. I dialed him back on his cell phone and he was so excited to hear from me. He told me that he was talking on his brand new I-Phone that Jeff had gotten him. We talked for a few minutes and he told me that he loved me and that he'd call me after he got in from basketball practice.

I walked upstairs and wanted to avoid calling my lawyer back because I didn't want to deal with it because it hurt badly. I truly felt as if I hated Quentin because of what he had done to us. Even though I knew that we both played a part in the downfall of our marriage I wasn't willing to look at my part, I could only focus on that which my husband had done. I reluctantly called my lawyer because I didn't want to hear what he had to say. I dialed the number and to my surprise, I was rather shocked by what he had to say. Apparently, Quentin had his lawyer fax over a divorce settlement agreement, and he advised me that I needed to seriously consider his offer.

Quentin decided that he was going to give me all of the rental properties, the second car, the house, and half of all the investment income that he had earned while we were married. I was floored because apparently my husband was worth close to two million dollars. I was very intrigued by the offer, but I immediately came to my senses and told my lawyer that I was not going to settle for anything, I wanted to battle it out in court and make this Negro pay. How in the hell could he try to buy me off? Did he think that the money would excuse his behavior? I had to make sure that he paid for everything; I was going to make sure that this thing ended nasty and that he walked away with nothing because there was no way I was going to allow him and another woman to live the life of luxury. He was not getting off that easy and I was serious about that one. I told my lawyer to reject the offer and inform his lawyer that we were going to see one another in court. I hung the phone up steaming mad because I could not believe that this fool had the audacity to try and buy me off. Was he foolish enough to think that I was crazy enough to take his offer? I picked up the phone and called his cell. He quickly answered, "Hello, Chelsi…what's up?"

I said, "Yeah, I got the offer that you sent over to my lawyer and I just wanted to let you know that I rejected it. You're a fucking idiot! A real piece of work! You aint shit! You must be crazy to think that I'd settle. We began to have a little shouting match back and forth and then I heard a child in the background say "Daddy, who is that, why are you yelling? Is that Mommy?"

I was stunned and shocked because he was really playing the good papa role. I was infuriated, and I told him that I was going to see his weak ass in court and that he needed to be prepared for the battle of his life. I hung up in his ear and I started to think about how I was going to make him pay big time. I was going to get everything I was entitled to; he was going to wish he'd never done anything like this to me. I was going to make sure that his lying, cheating, pathetic ass didn't have a pot to piss in or a window to throw it out of. He was going to be broke when I was finished. I felt so much anger and rage inside that I lost it.

I went into the huge his and hers closet that we shared in our master suite and I began to rip all of his clothes from the shelves...I grabbed a pair of scissors and cut his clothes up. There were five hundred-dollar suits and two hundred-dollar slacks in my path of destruction. I ran into his office and began to break all of his most prized and cherished awards that he'd received for business. I was about thirty minutes into my destruction spree and my cell phone rang. I looked at the caller ID and it was Malcolm's number! What did he want? Why was he calling me? I sat there, and I decided to hit ignore. I couldn't continue to see this man because he was married. I didn't want to continue to put myself out there and further lower myself to the standards of a classic booty call.

After the heated exchange of words that Quentin and I shared, I needed a drink. I wasn't usually one to drink often but alcohol and Malcolm seemed to be my cure-alls for the moment. I called my lawyer and made sure that I told him everything that had transpired, I told him about Quentin and his infidelity. I spilled it all! I told him of his children and I told him that he was taking care of his mistress with my money. I was like a shark in ocean waters looking for blood and was going to make sure that I got it, by any means necessary! He was going to be up the creek without a paddle and I was going to come out on top. There was no compromising with me and the price of my current pain was going to be more than my soon to be Ex-Husband would ever imagine.

Drunk and again overcome by my pain, I reached for my phone and returned the Malcolm's call. I told him that I needed to see him because we needed to talk. He chuckled insinuating that he knew that talking was not the only thing on my mind. I guess he could tell by my sloppy vocabulary, that I was in no shape to drive. He sent a car to pick me up and I eagerly anticipated my arrival to see him. After about 20 minutes, I arrived at his house. I stumbled to the door to find him there waiting for me. He helped me into the house and led me to his family room. I was impressed with the way he treated me and tried to care for me in my condition. I guess he realized that I was too incapacitated, and he decided to let me sleep for a while.

After a few hours I awoke to find Malcolm sitting across from the loveseat that I was laying on. He was watching CNN, or one of those national news channels. I walked over to him and sat beside him. He looked at me and said, "I see you're finally awake. I took the liberty of making a fresh pot of coffee, maybe you should drink it." I grabbed a cup and filled it halfway, the coffee immediately gave me a burst of energy, and the sluggishness from all the alcohol that I had consumed was slowly wearing off. I looked over at Malcolm and asked him, if he'd just lay with me and hold me. I didn't need to have sex with him; all I needed was to be held. I needed to feel like I was more than an expendable sex object. I wanted to feel like a woman who was wanted, needed, and loved by a man. I knew that he didn't love me, and I knew that I didn't love him, but the illusion of love was better than having nothing at all. He told me that he'd hold me, and he did. We laid there on the floor of his family room, in front of the fireplace, wrapped in the comfort of one another's bodies. We were there together and neither of us had any expectations or demands...though our bodies craved more, we resisted the urge and renounced the physical requirements that had started our wrong relationship in the first place.

For one brief moment I felt as if Malcolm and I were something more. It was as if he and I shared a bond, one that was unbreakable. In our delusional reality of the moment he was special to me and I was special to him, no matter if it was just for a brief moment in time. Again, he gave me just what I needed, and I melted from the warmth of his body, and found myself at peace once more in the arms of another woman's husband, a man that I barely knew.

CAUGHT RED HANDED
(KYRIA WILLIAMS)

After the amazing day in Key West with JD, we both knew that it was time to return home and face the reality of our situation. I finally got up enough nerve to tell him about the threat that Malcolm had made. He told me not to worry and that everything was really going to be ok. We packed our things and told Adella goodbye. I felt bad because she had grown so attached to Justin. She kissed his little face and kissed his little hands and told him that she loved him very much. It was really a rather sweet moment because you could see all the love in this woman's face. Adella was an amazing mother and grandmother and I was glad to have her in Justin's life. JD and I said our goodbyes and we boarded the plane to return to Indianapolis.

The flight was rather quiet. I guess I was a little tense because I really didn't want to have to face Malcolm and all of his hatefulness. JD asked me if I wanted to talk. I told him no because I really didn't know what to say. My mind was a jumbled mess. I felt as if I was going to lose it at any moment.

I looked over at JD as he was holding Justin; he looked a little scared as if he thought he was going to lose him. I asked him if he was ok and if wanted to talk about anything, but he said no and that he just wanted to continue to enjoy the time that he had left with his son. We decided that we were going to leave the airport separately and that I was going to call him once Justin and I were home and settled. There was no way I was going to deal with Malcolm alone, he had the worst temper and I didn't know how he would react to the news that I was leaving him, and that Justin was not his son.

We landed, and it was time for us to go our separate ways. I looked into JD's eyes and he looked into mine. He told me again that everything was going to be alright; he grabbed our bags and walked me and Justin to the car that was waiting outside of the airport. After strapping Justin's car seat into the car, he said goodbye and that he'd talk to me later and walked away. The driver began to slowly drive away, but suddenly stopped. I looked out the window and then saw JD was running toward the car, he opened the door grabbed me by the hand and pulled me out of the car and said, "Kyria, baby listen, I love you so much. I know that this is crazy and you're probably terrified, but I promise you that I am going to protect you from any pain. I want you to trust me with your heart and trust me with everything that you have, will you trust me?" I told him yes, I would and that I loved him too. He kissed me with the most passion that he'd ever kissed me with. I felt as if our souls were interconnected and joined the moment that our lips touched. I could feel his love for me in his kiss. His embrace was warm and comforting and I felt as if I was safe and that there was nothing that I had to worry about.

After the wonderful kiss from JD, I felt a little more empowered and equipped to deal with our situation. The ride from the airport was a little long and lonely without him, but I knew that we'd see one another soon. I looked over at Justin and he was sleeping so peacefully. I smiled because I was so happy that he couldn't understand the chaos that was about to come all because of his paternity. I was glad to be dealing with this, because this secret was killing me inside. We finally pulled up to the house. I didn't call Malcolm because I hoped that he was at work. I grabbed my bags and Justin. We walked in the door, and I went into the family room to put Justin in his swing. I was shocked to find Malcolm and some strange woman sleeping in the floor!

I yelled, "What in the hell is going on here? Malcolm you have to be kidding me!" The woman was startled and looked like she was terrified of what I was going to do to her. Malcolm got up unbothered, with a smug arrogant look on his face. "Don't you bring your ass up here in my house talking to me like you are crazy? You decided because you didn't get your way you wanted to run out of town, I was tired of playing this cat and mouse game with you. She is my guest and she doesn't have to leave. Chelsi, this is my ghetto fabulous, hood rat wife Kyria!" I looked at him like he was crazy. The woman decided that she was going to excuse herself and abruptly left, saying that she was so sorry. I stood there looking as Malcolm looked down on me like he was better than me.

"Well Malcolm I am so glad that you decided that you wanted to cheat, I truly hope you got what you wanted and needed." He chuckled, wickedly, and said, "Oh yes she was great! Much better than your fat ass! Kyria let's move on, I'm glad you came to your senses and brought your pretty face home. What are you cooking for dinner tonight?" I guess this fool thought that I was going to take his crap. This dude was fucking crazy to think that I was going to stay with him after catching him laid up with some random woman. I said, "Malcolm, Justin and I are leaving. There is no way I am stay here with you after all of this. I want a divorce." He smirked and looked at me, walking closer as if he was going to hit me. He grabbed me forcefully and said, "Listen you ungrateful hood rat whore....you can leave and take that got-damned hollering ass baby with you! I didn't ask you to get pregnant with him. I didn't want any more kids! I got my kids and I'm not paying any high ass child support for another one. So, if you go, just know you aint getting a damned thing from me. You can't take anything that you got while married to me; I want you to leave with just what you came with NOTHING! I gave you everything that you have; I took your ass out of the projects and gave you a life that you would never have been able to afford. You didn't even have any etiquette or class. I made you bitch! You knew nothing, and I transformed you from an ignorant, young project chick to a classy, high society woman. You are nothing without me and there is no way that you will ever be anything without me. I'm sure that you don't want to go back to where you came from! How you gonna eat? How you gonna get a job? You have nothing more than a GED, you are trash! How are you gonna feed that baby? You will be back, but better yet I bet your gold digging ass won't walk out that door. You love the money...right?"

I was overcome by tears as I listened to my husband talk to me like I was the scum of the earth. I thought this man loved me to some degree, but there was no way that he could love me and speak to me in such a hateful and awful way. Oh, and the things he said about my son! I knew that he had no connection with Justin, but that was horrible. I stood there trying to compose myself because I was going to make this Negro squirm. He was going to eat every word when I told him the truth. I sat there and began to laugh hysterically. I walked out of the room and grabbed my cell phone; I sent JD a text and told him that Justin and I were coming to his house and he needed to get here now.

I returned to the room where Malcolm was sitting and said, "Well, now that you have gotten the truth off of your chest, let me return the favor. You think that you made me, but that isn't the case. You are a controlling, manipulative, snake tongue, cheating, lying bastard. While you think that you have been getting over on me, I have actually been the one getting over on you. I put up with your foolishness and your hatefulness, not because I had nothing better to do, but because I wanted a better life for myself. I may not be the perfect woman for you but trust me I am the perfect woman for someone else. I am tired of you and as far as me needing you; I don't need anything from you! Everything that you gave me you can keep it buddy. I will be glad to rid myself of you. I'm so glad that you decided to show your true colors. I'm glad that you were able to get all of your true feelings off of your chest. You are nothing more than a forty something washed up, bully, who uses your money to try and make yourself look big, because you are trying to compensate for your lack in other areas. You can't even keep it up long enough! You think that you have me backed into a corner, but you don't. You don't have to worry about my son, because guess what Boo...he's not yours! His father is ten times the man you will ever be. So guess what? Fuck you Malcolm!"

He walked toward me as I was trying to leave the room and grabbed me by my arm. "What did you just say about Justin? He's not mine...I know that I didn't hear you say that?" I snatched away from him and told him, "Yeah you heard me right, he's not yours mutha-fucka! But that should be relief to you considering the fact that you care nothing about him!" He raised his hand and tried to hit me, and JD came bursting through the door. His dominant voice echoed in the room! "I dare you put your hands on her man and I'm gonna put my hands on you!" Malcolm looked over at JD, and said, "JD what the hell are you doing here? Man look, this doesn't have anything to do with you!" JD laughed, "Yeah man this has a whole lot to do with me...you see last year when you were busy working and mistreating her, she met me in Miami. We shared a wonderful two weeks together and Justin is my son! She doesn't deserve to be treated like a dog, no woman does! It's punk ass men like you that give good brothas like me a bad name. Kyria is beautiful and amazing and so intelligent. If you would have spent time getting to know her and appreciating her then maybe you'd see what I see. I love her; I came to get her and my son, it's time for them to be with me where they belong! You think that you are king, but you're nothing dude, just a punk ass, old school wanna be player. I didn't know that she was coming back to Indianapolis to be treated like this and if I'd known she would have stayed right there in Miami with me last year and would have been free of you long ago. I'm taking her and my son back home with me, and if you call her or even try anything, I'm gonna break you down and expose you for the coward that you are. If you think I'm playing, I dare you to try me. I will show you that you ain't as hard as you think. Don't let this Armani suit fool you bruh, I'll fuck you up about mine. Oh yeah, and by the way man, I suggest you try and find someone else to help fund your new firm, because I'm out...here's your chump change back...with your shady, bitch ass!"

He tossed twenty-five thousand dollars in cash onto the floor in front of Malcolm's feet, he looked over at me and said, "Come on baby, let's go." He grabbed Justin and grabbed my hand and we walked out of the door. I was bubbling over on the inside because JD came in there and shut it down! I couldn't believe that he gave the money back and was walking away from such a lucrative business deal. I didn't know what the deal was going to entail, but financially I knew that it would result in a great deal of money.

After getting into the car, I asked JD was he sure that he wanted to walk away from the business, and he said, "Yes, you and my son mean more to you than all the money in the world. What does it matter when you have a fortune with no one to share it with? Besides, I heard from a colleague of mine that Malcolm has been caught up in some shady business deals and he's about to lose it all because of scandal. I am an honest working man. I built my business from the ground up, with integrity and I can't afford to have my name caught up in scandal." I smiled at him and felt overcome with emotion, I leaned over and kissed him and told him that I loved him. I was so relieved to be with him, I knew that he loved me. I didn't know what was going to happen with JD and me, but I was looking forward to the infinite possibilities.

CHOOSE YOUR WORDS WISELY
(MARISSA KINCAID)

It had been quite some time since Robert and the girls left. I was getting a little concerned because there was no sign of them. I tried calling his cell, but it went straight to voicemail. I figured he was purposely doing that because he was mad at me. I really hated that he was upset. I wasn't trying to make him mad, but I was trying to just express what I was feeling. He never took an overly serious tone with me like he did today. He was always so easy going and very silly at times. I couldn't help but notice that daylight was fading rather quickly, and I tried to call him again, there was still no answer. I paced the floor and really started to get worried, and an awful feeling had come over me. Instantly, I knew that something was terribly wrong.

It was at that exact moment that I was overcome with this gut wrenching feeling, my cell phone rang, and the caller ID said the number was restricted. I answered, and it was Chelsi, "Hello Marissa it's Chelsi"...I thought to myself what does she want? I don't have time for her drama, not now. I answered,

"Yes Chelsi, how can I help you? If you are looking for Robert, he is out with the girls!" She said, "Actually, that's what I'm calling about, ummm I don't know how to tell you this, but there was a terrible accident, Quentin… lost control of the car and slammed into a tree. He and the girls have been life-lined to St. Vincent's Hospital, it's pretty bad. You should get here right away!"

I was speechless. There was lump the size of a golf ball that formed in my throat. I couldn't think straight. I was numb all over. I grabbed Brayden and ran to the car and drove to St. Vincent. I was so afraid because I didn't know what to expect when I got there. I tried my best to remain calm because I had to focus and drive. After the longest 20 minutes of my life I arrived at the hospital. I grabbed Brayden out of his car seat and ran into the emergency department information desk. I told the lady that I was looking for a man and two little girls that were brought in by Life-Line. She told me to have a seat and that someone from the care team would come and speak to me. I sat down and a tall slender, middle aged man appeared before me. He said, "Are you here for Mr. Adams and the Adams children?" I said yes, and he asked me to follow him and we walked into a conference room. I didn't know what he was going to say…was he going to tell me that they were dead? What was he going to say? He proceeded to tell me that both Arianna and Brianna were saved by their booster seats; he said that they were both awake upon arrival, but very disoriented and extremely hysterical. They were given mild sedatives to calm them down for their examinations, and for the battery of tests that needed to be run. He said that they suffered a few cuts and bruises to their faces and that they both had bruised ribs and fractured collarbones, but other than that they were ok. He told me that they were both taken to the pediatric ICU and that I could see them at any time. Then I asked about Robert, and with a look of concern, he told me that Robert had extensive internal injuries, and severe head trauma and he had to be immediately rushed into surgery to stop the bleeding. He said they had removed his spleen and a lobe of his liver. He had a broken collarbone, a broken leg, a fractured eye orbit, and a collapsed lung. He told me that Robert's heart stopped once while he was on the operating table, but they were able to revive him quickly.

I asked him if Robert was going to die and he said that the next 24 hours were going to be crucial. He had lost a significant amount of blood, and even though he was an active and healthy, young man, his body suffered a tremendous amount of shock. He was unconscious upon arrival and hadn't regained consciousness yet. He was still rather critical, but they were cautiously optimistic. We just needed to wait. He told me that his name was Dr. Wiesenberger and that he was in charge of the girls and Robert's care and that if I had any questions to please not hesitate to call him. He told me that the nurse would show me to the girl's room and that Robert was on a different floor from them. I asked the nurse if they had a volunteer that could help with Brayden. She said yes and that I could go and see the girls and she'd keep Brayden until they could find a helper that was on call.

I walked into the room and there were both of my girls. There little heads bandaged and their little faces all battered and bruised. Their pretty little faces were covered with little scrapes and drops of dried blood; I could see little fine pieces of shattered glass in their little ponytails. My heart was broken. I began to cry because I was so angry that this happen. How could Robert be so careless? How did he lose control of the car? Why my babies? I reached over the rail of the bed and rubbed Brianna's head, she was laying there looking helpless. I hurt so much because there was nothing that I could do. I kissed her little face and told her that Mommy loved her. I walked over to Arianna and did the same thing. The tears were heavily flowing from my eyes and I felt as if I was having a nervous breakdown.

After about two minutes of heavy sobbing, I heard Arianna's little broken and weak voice, "Mommy, why are you crying?" I was elated to hear her voice and ran over to her little bed. "Oh baby, hi baby! Mommy's ok. How are you feeling, don't try and talk ok, just rest." She smiled and said ok and she drifted back to sleep. I called the nurse and asked her if Brayden was ok, and she said yes, he was fine.

I told her that I was going to see Robert and if the girls needed me to please call me on my cell. I kissed the girls on their foreheads and headed up the elevator to see Robert. I walked into the room and was intimidated by the many tubes, wires, monitors and IV fluid bags. There was a small stool next to the bed, and I sat there. Robert was in bad shape, and nothing could ever have prepared me to see him like this. I began to cry, and his nurse walked in, she said hi and rubbed my back. She told me to try and calm myself and that he was doing ok considering. She said that his vitals were stable for the moment and that if I needed her to please ring the call light. I thanked her, and she left the room. I scooted myself up to Robert and laid my head on the bed next to his discolored, battered, and swollen face. He was so bruised and puffy that I almost didn't recognize him. I whispered in his ear, "Robert baby I'm here...please wake up you have to get better, the girls, Brayden and I need you."

I touched his hand and I hoped that he could hear me because he moved his arm. I grabbed his hand and kissed it. I hoped that he would open his eyes. I just wanted to see his beautiful brown eyes...I wanted him to know that I was there. There he was, this beautiful, strong man, lying there helpless and fragile, broken and battered. This man that was so huge to me was now so small and reduced to the most weakened and vulnerable state that I'd ever seen him in. My heart was further tormented because I couldn't do anything to help. I couldn't do anything but sit there and watch the man I love fight for his life.

I called down to check on the girls they were still sleeping. I decided that I needed to do something that I hadn't done in a while. I walked out of the room and walked to the elevator. I followed the wall signs and directories to the first floor of the hospital to the Chapel. I walked into the beautiful Chapel and went and knelt down in front of the makeshift altar. I looked up to the ceiling and began to talk to God.

"Lord...it's me Marissa. I know that I haven't talked to you in a while, and I know that I don't deserve to ask you for anything. I'm not coming here on my behalf, but I'm coming on the behalf of my children. I ask that you please heal Robert, not for me, but my kids. They need their father God...they need him. I know that we have not done right in your eyes, and I'm so sorry to have let you down. I know you, and I love you, and I know better. I just ask that you please have mercy on Robert, have mercy on me and bring him back. Please Lord...please don't let him die....please don't." I burst into tears and fell on my face. I remembered in that moment how my Father used to explain the grace and mercy of God. Robert and I both needed his grace and we both needed his mercy. I prayed for God to move in a way that only he could. I got up

from the altar and sat in the front row. I then felt a
light touch on my shoulder and turned to find Chelsi
standing there. She looked like she had been crying
and asked if she could talk to me. I really didn't want
to talk to her because I was afraid that we'd argue,
and I didn't want any drama. I reluctantly agreed to
listen to her. That was the least that I could do
considering the situation. I sat there and listened to
her. She told me that she was sorry because she felt
as if this was her fault. Apparently, she had been
arguing with Robert right before the accident.

"Marissa, I was so angry and I had been drinking
and I just wanted to let him know how much I hated
what he had done to us. I never intended to cause
such a tragedy, and when I got the call from the
police, I felt so horrible. Look I know that you
probably will hate me for telling you this, but I hope
that you will understand that I never wanted
anything bad to happen to your children. I never
wanted those kids to hurt. I have a son, and I would
never wish anything like this on another Mother."
She told me that she was planning to cause so many
problems and fight the divorce, but when this
happened, she realized how precious life is and that
in an instant things can change. She told me that it
wasn't worth it, and that she understood why Robert
fell in love with me. She said their marriage was over
long before I came into the picture. She pushed him
away and he ran to where he could be comforted
and that was with me. She told me that she was not
going to fight anything; She was going to give

Robert his divorce uncontested and agree to the terms offered by his attorney.

I sat there speechless, because I wanted to hate her for making him distracted to the point of him losing control of the car and nearly killing my children, but I couldn't. I guess in a way I kind of respected her for being the better person. I admired her for taking the high road and stepping to me like an adult. I reached out and grabbed her hand and told her that I forgave her and that I prayed that she would forgive me too. "Chelsi, I never meant to hurt you. I didn't seek to destroy your marriage or cause any problems. I never wanted to bring this kind of pain to anyone. We made a mistake and got caught up and for that, I'm truly sorry. Regardless of the state of your marriage, you didn't deserve this pain. No one does. I can't help but think that maybe this is my Karma. Maybe this is mine and Roberts karma." I hugged her and told her that I was so sorry. She said that it was fine and that she needed to do the right thing, and she was not going to cause any problems. I thanked her, and she turned and walked away. I asked her to please go and see Robert; she told me that she couldn't bear to see him that way. I said ok and watched as she walked away.

I didn't really know how to take things; it was crazy, like something straight off of Lifetime TV. I gathered my thoughts and walked from the Chapel and returned to the girl's room. I called the nurse and asked for Brayden, and I sat there in the rocking chair, with my infant son, watching my daughters sleeping, while praying for their father. Praying that he would be alive in the morning when we woke up.

SOMETIMES THE RIGHT THING TO DO IS THE HARDEST (CHELSI ADAMS)

It had been a long and very emotional day. I tried hard to forgive myself because I felt responsible for what happened to Quentin and his children. I really could not imagine the fear in Marissa when she got the phone call. I really wanted to be there to support Quentin after all, he was still my husband, but the guilt was taking a toll on me. I could not bear to see this man fighting for his life. I couldn't help but think that maybe he wouldn't be in this situation if I hadn't called and started an argument with him. I let my anger and rage consume me and I spiraled out of control because of my emotions. My fight to save my marriage was selfish because the reality of this situation is that this marriage is over and has been over for quite some time. We could have fought for it but neither of us wanted to. There are just some things that relationships can't recover from and apparently the things that we had been through proved too challenging for us to conquer.

I walked into the house and stared around at the broken glass and torn fabrics from my destructive emotional rampage that I went on earlier in the afternoon. I began to cry when I saw all the damage that I had done. I grabbed the broom and the dust pan and began to clean up after myself. I felt awful because there wasn't a shred of viable clothing of Quentin's left in the closet. I had destroyed everything. After about forty-five minutes my path of debris was cleared and there was some sense of normalcy to the room. I picked up my phone and called Jeff, it was time for me to tell him to prepare Alex for the news. I dialed his number and after about two rings he answered. "Hey, Chelsi what's up?" I said, "Hey Jeff, are you busy at the moment? I need to talk to you." He told me that he wasn't busy and that we could talk. I told him that there had been a terrible accident and that Quentin was in the hospital fighting for his life. He asked me if I needed him to come down, and I told him no. I guess that he could tell that there was more on my mind and he asked me if there was something else. I sat there silent, holding the phone and tears started to roll down my face. Jeff said, "Chelsi...what's wrong, talk to me?" I broke down and told him everything, I told him that Quentin and I had been having problems for some time and that we were getting a divorce. I told him about Marissa and the kids, I told him about Malcolm, I told him about the argument and that the little girls were in the car and injured also. Jeff sat there on the phone speechless. After a few moments he finally just said with a tone of shock, "Wow, Chelsi, I don't know what to say. I can't believe that all of that has happened. I know that you are hurting, but it looks like to me that you allowed yourself to spiral out of control, and that isn't you. I can't imagine being in such a situation, but you must pull yourself together. Look I am not the relationship expert, but I know what it is like to make mistakes that cost you your relationship, I did it with you. But you have to accept that things are over and move on. And stop selling yourself short emotionally."

It was good to talk to Jeff. He was always so candid and transparent, and he had a nonjudgmental spirit. I knew that he would tell me the truth and also listen to me and try to see things from my perspective. He told me that he would tell Alex about the accident, but not about anything else. I told him that I appreciated him for listening and talking through things with me.

We said our goodbyes and hung up the phone. I decided that I was going to call my lawyer. I called him and told him about the accident and informed him that I wanted to stick with the original divorce settlement. I asked him to change one thing though; I told him that I didn't want any of the investment income. I told him that I was sure that Quentin would need it because he had a long recovery ahead of him. My lawyer asked me if I was sure, and I told him yes. I hung up the phone and set on the side of my bed, tears were streaming down my face because I still couldn't believe that my marriage was over. The events of the last day were something that I never expected. I had to take time and regroup. As I sat there my cell phone rang, I noticed that it was Marissa.

I answered the phone immediately because I was afraid that something had happened to Quentin. "Hello, Marissa is everything ok?" She cried, "No, Chelsi, Robert......ummmm....Quentin needs a blood transfusion and they need to take him back into surgery because he is bleeding internally. I can't consent to anything because I'm not his wife. Could you please come....please hurry and come!" I told her yes and rushed back to the hospital to do what would be the last thing that I would ever do as Quentin's wife.

OUT WITH THE OLD....IN WITH THE NEW (KYRIA WILLIAMS)

After the confrontation with Malcolm, JD and I walked into his beautiful condo. He told me that he had a surprise for me. We walked down the hallway to one of three rooms of off the living room. He told me to open the door, and I opened the door and it was a nursery. The walls were painted baby blue, and, on the ceiling, there was a mural that looked like the clear, star filled night sky. There was the most beautiful crib that was decorated with a custom-made crib set that had Justin's name stitched into it. The room had a rocking chair and changing table that matched the crib. On the wall above the head of the crib there were letters that spelled out Justin's name. I was mesmerized because it was perfect. I grabbed JD and kissed him and told him thank you and I loved the nursery. He told me that he just wanted Justin to be comfortable. I felt like I was still dreaming because this man was nothing like

what I was used to. We walked back into the living
room and JD grabbed Justin and took him into his
beautiful new nursery and put him in his crib.

I grabbed my phone and called a lawyer that was
recommended by JD to me. I told him my situation
and that I needed to file for a divorce. I told him
that I didn't want anything from Malcolm, I wanted
to cut all ties to him. He asked me if I was sure and I
said yes. After speaking to the lawyer, he told me
that he'd prepare the necessary paperwork. I asked
him about a retainer and he told me that he'd had
already been given a retainer. Apparently, JD paid
the retainer fee. I couldn't believe that he had done
this for me. I knew that when I told Malcolm that I
was leaving that he was going to cancel all of my
bank and credit cards. I knew that I was going to be
broke, but that didn't matter because I just wanted
to be happy.

I held myself captive for all this time because I
was scared to let go of what I thought I had. I came
from poverty and the life of luxury was so easy and
carefree. I was tired of suffering and being driven by
money. I wanted to be driven by love. Love and
respect means more than money and I had that with
JD. We had a mutual love and respect for one
another. I went into the bathroom and decided that I
was going to take a shower. I removed my clothes
and stepped into the luxury glass door shower. It
was so nice it had beautiful brushed nickel fixtures
and it was lined with the loveliest, earth toned,

travertine tiles. I stood under the stream of the water and fell in love with the feel of its warmth against my skin. I was so relaxed and felt like I could stay there all day.

I saw JD walk into the bathroom and he asked me if he could join me. I smiled and said yes. He stepped into the shower and I looked at his beautiful body. He was so fine. I mean he was everything that any woman can ask for. He grabbed me and pulled me closely and began to kiss me, he grabbed the wash towel and washed every part of my body and I gladly returned the favor. After about 15 minutes of showering together we stepped out of the shower, and JD picked me up in his arms and took me into the bedroom. He looked into my eyes and told me that he was going to make love to me. He laid me on the bed and began exploring my body with his mouth and hands. I was taken away by his sweet kisses and his gentle touch. Our bodies were locked and loaded, and the emotions were running high. JD continued his pursuit of loving me. His manhood danced freely in the comfort of my love, and I surrendered to sweet ecstasy. JD was amazing, and I wanted him to continue to give freely of himself. My hips danced to the glide and groove of his stroke and beat. With every minute we gained more intensity and more emotion. I could feel the force building inside my body as he was guided himself deeper into the sweetness that was within me. Feeling that he was nearing his launch into the realm of total satisfaction, I held him tighter; I squeezed him harder in my attempt to help him reach his peak of excitement. Fueled by the actions of my body, he quickened his stroke and eventually his body became still and motionless. He held me tightly and I could feel the power being released from deep within the depths of his beautiful body. His breathing was heavy…while attempting to speak…his words were broken, and I knew that he was there…just where I wanted him to be. He kissed me and told me that I was the best thing that ever happened to him. I smiled, glad that I was able to fulfill the needs of this man whom I loved so much. I laid there in his arms wishing that the moment could never end; I wanted to capture this time in my life and frame it.

There we lay together, more than a year after our first encounter in Miami. Who would have imagined that we'd be together again? Who would have known that I would be able to rid myself of the awful secret of my son's paternity? I had escaped from a relationship that was built on the wrong things. I let money and luxury blind me, and I traded real love for it. Coming from the hood, having to struggle can cause you to do some strange things for some change. I can now say that there is no amount of money that is ever worth compromising yourself and being mistreated.

Even though JD and I didn't get here the right way, we were here together. I never loved any man like I loved him, and no other man has ever loved and treated me like he does. He is a wonderful man. He is strong and intelligent. He is a great father and a great provider. He is the one thing that I truly needed in my life and having him made me finally believe in love at first sight. I don't know what tomorrow holds for JD and me, but I will continue to live in the moment and love him one day at a time.

I'LL KEEP HOLDING ON
(MARISSA KINCAID)

Thankful that Chelsi had returned to the hospital to sign the consent for Robert's blood transfusion and surgery, I sat waiting for the doctors to return. Chelsi sat across from me. We barely said anything to one another, even though we'd spoken our peace it wasn't like we'd instantly become friends. I called up to the nurses' station on the Pediatric ICU floor to check up on the girls. Their nurse told me that they were fine, they had both woke up for a few minutes but went back to sleep. She said that they would probably sleep for a while because they still had elevated levels of the sedatives in their systems. I said ok and asked her to please let me know if things were to change. I was holding Brayden and he had begun to play a little bit he sat on my lap and babbled in his baby talk. I laughed as he tried to put his fingers in my mouth. I said, "I don't want to eat your fingers Pooh, Mama doesn't want any." I kissed his fat juicy jaws. His little face lit up brightly and he bellowed out the biggest and cutest laugh. I tried to not notice Chelsi as she was sitting over across from me, but it was hard to ignore the look of disgust on her face. She tried to not look at me or Brayden and I could tell that she was really bothered.

We sat there for a few hours waiting to get word of the progress of Robert's surgery. I walked over and sat next to Chelsi and asked her if we could talk. She nodded yes, and I said, "Look Chelsi I know that this is hard for you and I want you to know that I really appreciate you for being here with me. I know that I am not your favorite person, but I want to thank you because of my children." She looked at me, with tears in her eyes, "You know Marissa; I have to admit that I really don't care for you. I'm not doing this because I care about you or your happiness. We are not friends and we will never be. The only thing that we have in common is the fact that we both happen to love the same man. I came here out of my obligation as a wife, and I also did this for your kids because my son has his father and I could not imagine how it would affect him if anything were to happen to him. I am not happy with why we are here, but I just want to do the right thing. I hope that your kids recover quickly, and that Quentin Robert Adams makes it to see another day, because this is not about you or me it's about those kids." We sat there staring at one another, tears falling steadily from both of our eyes. Here we were two women loving one man, two women living two totally different lives with this one man. He was Quentin to her and Robert to me. He was her husband and he was my lover...the father of my children. She had memories that were painful and bad, while most of mine up to this moment were rather good. She saw him as something awful while I saw him as something wonderful. The both of us were here trying to do our part to help the man that we both loved. She was helping to close the door to her past while helping me to open the door to my future.

Finally, the nurse came out to give us a report on Robert's progress. She said that the surgery was going well, but they were being slowed down because he had a couple of bleeders that were a little harder to stop. She said that his vitals were stable and that considering his grave condition, he was fighting hard. She told us that he needed a platelet transfusion because his platelet count was very low. She said the doctors hoped to wrap the surgery up soon and that she would keep us posted on any additional information. I sat there hoping that this nightmare would soon be over and that we'd be able to move forward with our lives.

Another hour had past and the nurse finally returned to tell us that they had just taken Robert into recovery. I had just returned from checking in on the girls. They were doing much better and seemed to be making pretty good progress. They were in a lot of pain, so the doctor told me that he really wanted to focus on their pain control. I had stayed with them until they returned to sleep and was going to go back once things were settled with their father. The nurse told us that we could see him in about forty-five minutes or so. I was going to go to the cafeteria to grab a bite to eat because I was feeling a bit light headed. I asked Chelsi if she wanted anything, she said no, but surprisingly she told me that she'd watch Brayden for me. I really didn't know what to say, but she insisted and said that it was ok. I handed Brayden to her, and she smiled at him and said, "Well hello there little guy! Wow you sure are a cutie." I walked out the door and left my baby in the arms of his father's wife. This was sure some crazy mess. I shook my head still feeling like I was in a bad dream

I returned from the cafeteria into the waiting room and Chelsi had a visitor. He was a tall, dark-skinned, man. He was rather good looking. I thought to myself did she invite her boyfriend here to wait with her? Who was this guy, and why does she have him here? I walked over to Chelsi and got Brayden I thanked her, and she introduced me to her friend. She said his name was Jeff and he was her son's father. I said hello and walked over to the seat across the room. It was a rather awkward moment because; it felt like the guy was watching me. It was like he knew who I was and had some negative impression of me.

I sat there watching as they had a conversation; at times they seemed to be whispering. I sure hoped that they weren't talking about me. I know that Robert and I were wrong for how things happened but the last thing I needed was someone judging me. The nurse came back in and said Mrs. Adams you can see your husband now." She looked at Chelsi, and Chelsi then looked at me with a smirk on her face. It was almost as if she was taunting me. Even though Robert and I were together, nothing could change the fact that she was still his wife and her privileges trumped mine.

THE TIME HAS COME TO LET GO
(CHELSI ADAMS)

I couldn't believe that I was sitting there holding her baby! What was wrong with me? I guess I was temporarily in sane, or maybe I was still feeling a little guilty because of the accident. I didn't know why I offered but I did. He was a cutie pie; he was his father's child. He had the same eyes as Quentin and the same nose too. His hair and skin were the exact color of his father's. He really didn't look too much like Marissa at all. I sat there looking into the face of this cute, little, innocent baby boy. He smiled and babbled and cooed at me and I did really enjoy playing peek-a-boo with him. He was a busy body. While I was waiting for Marissa to get back a visitor appeared in the waiting room. It was Jeff! I looked shocked and asked him what he was doing here. He smiled and hugged me and said, "I thought that you could use a little support right now. You sounded terrible on the phone and I could not leave you alone at a time like this." I smiled and told him thank you for his kindness. I said, "Where is Alex? Is he here too?" He said, "No he's still in Ohio with Mama. He has a big outing planned with his Spanish class and he wouldn't want to miss it; besides I didn't think that it was the right time to spring all of this stuff on him. Of course I told him about the accident but I didn't tell him the extent of Q's injuries."

I couldn't believe that Jeff had made the three and a half hour journey here to support me. It really shouldn't have been a shock to me, because Jeff was so sweet. He always had a huge heart and he often put others before himself. He also had mastered the gift of forgiveness. He wasn't a grudge holder and he seemed to be able to move past things much easier than most people. Even though our relationship as a couple ended rather painfully we still had a great parental and friend relationship in spite of it. We never argued or disagreed much and when we did, we seemed to know how to put our differences aside and work toward the best interest of our son. He said he couldn't believe I was holding that girls baby. He told me that I was a big person for what I was doing. He told me that he was proud of me for my efforts to be civil because he knew that I would have beat a trick down in the past. We chuckled and began to reminisce about the old days. We really strayed away from the discussion about Quentin though, because neither of us felt like it was the appropriate time or place to talk about the situation.

Marissa returned to the room and I introduced

her to Jeff. Jeff was very polite, but I knew he was thinking about everything that I had told him about her. She looked a little puzzled and I made sure to clarify that he was Alex's father. I gave her back the baby and returned to the seat next to Jeff. We continued our conversation and he would from time to time discreetly ask me questions about the type of woman she was. I told him that I really didn't know too much about her, and truthfully, I didn't care to know. The nurse walked into the waiting room and looked right at me saying, "Mrs. Adams you can see your husband now." I looked over at Marissa, as to say yeah bitch…I'm his wife and you're not. I could see that it bothered her because she had been parading around this hospital like she was his wife and not his mistress. I know it was petty, but I couldn't resist.

I followed her back into the postoperative recovery suites and walked into Quentin's room. He was all bandaged and bruised. There were countless tubes, wires and monitors. I walked over to his bed and touched his hand and immediately began to cry, because I felt so responsible for him being in this situation. I was angry with him, but never wanted him to be critically injured. I couldn't help but to think about how things used to be. I couldn't help in my mind but to return to the days when we were all that we needed. My thoughts went back a few days to the last time that we were at our house. I had said some mean and nasty things to him and I wished that I could take them back.

I sat down next to his bed and began to talk to him. I told him that I was so sorry for calling his phone and saying I hated him. I told him that I never wanted anything tragic to happen to him. I didn't really know if he could hear me, but I just wanted him to know I was sorry. I told him that I wasn't going to fight and that I just wanted him to get better. I reached into my purse and decided to sign the divorce paperwork. I cried as I took a pen and signed my name, because I knew that my signature made this the beginning of our official and lawful end. I folded the papers and placed them in a white letter envelope and wrote "For Quentin" on the outside of it. I also put a letter inside and tried to highlight some of the good memories that we had shared. Although we were currently in this situation, it wasn't always like this. I guess time just had a way of changing things and changing us. We fell apart and weren't able to be repaired.

I walked out of the room and gathered my composure; I went to the nurse's station and asked to speak with the doctor. He came and met me in the conference room and asked me if everything was ok. I told him the situation, and that Quentin and I were in the middle of a divorce. I informed him that Marissa was his current partner and that I was giving her authority to make any decisions on his behalf. I gave him a copy of the divorce paperwork and included an official letter that I had drawn up by my lawyer releasing myself from any decisions regarding his medical treatment and long-term care. Some would probably say that I was wrong but prior to this he had decided to move on and become a family with her and since she wanted to play the role, I thought it would be best for her to do so. He told me that he understood and that he'd put the paper work in the chart and notify the care team of the changes. I told him thank you and walked back into the waiting room. I told Jeff that I was ready, and I told Marissa to please keep me posted. She thanked me again for everything and Jeff and I walked out of the room.

Jeff followed me back to the house and we went inside. I immediately began to cry. It was over; I had walked away and released myself from any obligations to my husband. I put his care and life in the hands of another woman. I removed my rings and placed them on the coffee table. Tears covered my face. Jeff consoled me and told me that the most important thing that I needed to do was to worry about was getting myself together. I must admit that, it felt good to be comforted by someone who truly knew me, someone who wasn't trying to gain anything, but they were only trying to give of themselves. It took me back before our breakup and how Jeff was the most sensitive and caring man that I had ever met.

Don't get me wrong, he was no punk, but he was comfortable enough in his manhood to make himself vulnerable and transparent. He told me that maybe I needed to take some time away from the city to clear my mind and to find peace in the situation. He really had a good point. Maybe it would do me some good to leave for a while.

He suggested that I come to Ohio and stay there with him and Alex for a while. He said it would be good for Alex to see me and good for me to see him. Jeff was the sweetest thing and I was so grateful to have him as a friend. It seemed like he was always there when I needed him. He was my Knight in Shining Armor that always rescued me the princess from the dragon that was myself. I thought it over and decided that I was going to take Jeff up on his offer. I was going to take some time and focus on rebuilding my life. I was going to focus on healing my hurts and bettering myself. I needed to get back to the place where I was healthy mentally, emotionally, physically and spiritually. Having had broken spirits for some time, I needed a healthy dose of happiness. I needed a change of scenery, I needed an escape from the madness that had now consumed and become my life. I needed to take back control of my life and I was going to do it away from drama, away from stress, and away from Indianapolis.

ANOTHER ONE BITES THE DUST
(KYRIA WILLIMAS)

It had been a few months since I filed my divorce from Malcolm. Things were going great for JD and me. My lawyer called to let me know that my divorce was final, and I was so excited. Justin and I were in Miami with Adella. JD had flown back to Indy to finalize some business. He had decided that he was going to do business with the mutual friend that he and Malcolm shared. I hadn't talked to him because he had been in meetings all day. I knew that he was coming back later so I decided that I would wait and tell him the news then. Adella and I went shopping for baby clothes. Justin was getting so big. He was outgrowing everything. I loved spending time with Adella because she was such a great person. She had such a sweet spirit and was always encouraging and upbeat, and besides she was the epitome of a true diva. She was beautiful; I prayed that I'd look as good as she did at 65.

We returned to the house and I asked her if she'd mind keeping Justin for the night. I was eagerly anticipating JD's arrival. She agreed and told me that she'd love spending time with her grandson. I wanted to spend the night and early morning hours celebrating my freedom from the horrible farce of a marriage with Malcolm. I kissed Justin and told Adella goodbye and that I would see her tomorrow.

I drove to JD's condo and prepared a nice dinner for him. I knew that he'd be coming home soon. I lit candles and prepared our place settings out on the balcony, overlooking the beach. I wanted to go back to where it all began. I made sure that I had on the sexiest dress in the closet. I was looking good and I knew that JD was going to be glad to see me. It was about 8:15 and I heard JD's keys in the door. I sat on the couch waiting for him to walk through the door. He walked in and saw me sitting there all dolled up, and said, "Damn baby you look good! You sure are a sight for sore eyes!" I smiled and threw my arms around his neck and said, "I take it you missed me, hmmm?" He said, "Yeah you know I missed you." I kissed his sexy soft lips and ran my fingers through the waves in his hair. He picked me up and spun me around in the air, we laughed and enjoyed reacquainting our lips with one another's.

I told him that I had a special dinner planned and he needed to put his things down and get ready to eat. I grabbed his hand and led him to the balcony. It was perfect. The sounds of smooth jazz perfectly complimented the echoing sound of the waves crashing upon the shore. There was a nice bottle of wine and JD's favorite dessert...German Chocolate cake. I had Adella make it...special order for our special night. He asked me where Justin was, and I said he was with Adella. He laughed and said, "What are you up to? You never get a sitter for the night unless you are up to something." I smiled and said "Well, maybe I am and maybe I'm not." We continued our dinner and dessert and went back into the house. I told him to sit down on the couch and close his eyes. I grabbed the final divorce decree and handed to him and asked him to open his eyes. He said, "so it's official!" I said, "Yes baby it is". He laughed and said, "Well today must have been Malcolm's day for endings. He got brought up on charges for his shady business dealings and his company was shut down by the feds. He's in some deep shit babe. He's been misappropriating funds for years."

I sat there feeling a little happy because that was what he got for mistreating me. It was amazing to me how in a blink of an eye everything was gone. I said "Oh well, looks like the mighty have fallen. You know they say the bigger they are the harder they fall. Please let's change the subject. Jayson Davis I am so happy that we are here together. I never would have imagined that you and I would be so much in love. You and Justin are the best things that have happened to me ever in my life. I want to spend every day of my life making you happy. I want to build my future with you. I see myself loving you until I take my last breath. I know this is not the way this goes but I have something to ask you. I pulled out a ring and got on one knee and I flipped the script and I proposed to him, "Jayson Alexander Davis will you marry me?" He sat there stunned with the biggest smile on his face. He said, "I'd be honored to marry you baby...yes I will!" He kissed me and held me tightly. He whispered in my ear, "I never want to let you go. I promise to make you happy for the rest of your life. I love you Kyria."

He carried me to the balcony and said, "Let's do it like we did the first-time baby." I was elated, and my body was too. He gave himself to me unlike he'd ever done before, and I took him all in. We tossed, turned and moved our bodies to provide maximum pleasure to the other. His lips explored my body and mine explored his. JD's body felt good mixed with mine and I knew that his eruption was nearing because his pace changed, and he was more precise in his movement. He was on a mission to pleasure me and I was on a mission to in return pleasure him. He was diving deeper and deeper until he reached that sweet spot. I lost control. Without warning, he exploded within the deepness of my body. I reacted to him and my body then produced orgasmic aftershocks. He rested there in my arms exhausted. He continued to kiss me and whisper how much he loved me and that he was so glad that I was going to be his wife.

We laid there together looking up at the stars, in

our own perfect paradise. JD told me he needed to say something, "Kyria I have everything that a man could ever want I knew when I first saw you that we belonged together. I knew that you were going to be mine from the start and when I made love to you for the first time I felt something that I had never felt for any other woman. Thank you for loving me and taking the chance to follow your heart. I am going to give you and Justin the world and hopefully soon we can give him a playmate."

I smiled and rolled over to my side reaching my hand under the blanket. I said well, maybe we can give him one sooner than you think. How does 8 months sound?" I handed him the pregnancy test with a big bold yes in the test window. He looked at me beaming and said, "Are you for real? You're pregnant?" I said "Yes I'm for real. His face lit up like the summer sky on the fourth of July. I was so glad to see the smile on his face. I never had the chance to have the man that I loved celebrate my pregnancy. JD wanted me, Justin and this baby and I was overjoyed. Neither of us would ever have thought that months go we'd be here. My life had taken a turn for the better and I felt so fortunate and thankful.

So here I was the girl who came from nothing, and now I had everything. Life could only continue to get better from this point. I walked into the house from the balcony and slipped on my bathrobe. JD walked in behind me.

There was a knock at the door. I opened the door

and was quickly pushed aside. Two police officers rushed in yelling, "Jayson Davis, you're under arrest!"

THE ROAD TO RECOVERY
(MARISSA KINCAID)

It had been several weeks since the terrible accident. Arianna and Brianna were progressing quite well. Their physical injuries had healed but the emotional trauma of such an accident was something we were all learning to deal with every day. The girls were very excited because their daddy was finally coming home. I was glad that he was coming home too. It was rather hard trying to take care of the kids and always find time to be there at the hospital. I loaded the kids in the car and made my way to pick up Robert.

When I arrived, went into the main door and called to the nurse's station and told them I was waiting outside for him. I didn't bother taking the kids out of the car because that would have been too much of a hassle, besides we weren't going to be up there long. After about ten minutes the nurse appeared pushing Robert in a wheelchair. She gave me his release paperwork and belongings. She helped him into the car and we were on our way. Robert was very happy to see the kids and they spent the entire car ride talking about everything he had missed. He looked over at me and smiled and mouthed thank you.

We pulled up to the house and the girls were excited for their Daddy to see their rooms. During his hospital stay we moved from the old condo to the new house Robert had purchased prior to the accident. Since the divorce was final Chelsi had ownership of the rental properties and decide to sell them. Robert was so happy to be home. He was still a little weak, but he was doing well. He went through extensive physical therapy because of his severely broken leg. He still was wearing a brace to give him some extra support for a while. He suffered some severe nerve damage and structure damage, so it is difficult for him to walk. There were many nights that were touch and go and we almost lost him a few times. He lost a tremendous amount of blood. He suffered swelling on his brain and had undergone a procedure to reduce the pressure. It was certainly a blessing that he was still with us.

We made our way into the house and I told him to have a seat, and rest. Arianna and Brianna both were hanging all over him. I got the kids settled and helped Robert up the stairs. As we were walking down the hall he said that he loved me. I told him that I loved him too. We made our way into the master suite and I was attempting help him sit on the bed and we lost our balance. I fell on top of him onto the bed. I was afraid that I hurt him and tried to get up quickly, but he wrapped his arms tightly around me and said, "Baby please don't get up." He kissed me, and I felt warm inside. It had been such a long time since he touched or kissed me. I was momentarily stuck in the moment, but quickly came to myself. I got up and said, "Ok baby, let me get up. I don't want to hurt you." I went to get the kids ready for bed and told him that I'd be back to help him get a shower and get ready for bed. I bathed the kids and I tucked them in and gave them kisses goodnight. The girls were a little sad because I told them that Robert wasn't going to be able to read their bedtime story to them. Surprisingly, when I walked out of Arianna's room Robert was slowly heading into Brianna's room.

After reading Arianna her bedtime story, he kissed her and made his way through the Jack and Jill bathroom to Brianna's room and did the same. He then made his way to Brayden's room and kissed him goodnight. I watched as he limped and struggled down the long hallway and was overjoyed with his determination concerning his kids. I was appreciative of his devotion to his role as a father. He made his way back to the bedroom and immediately asked for pain meds. I started fussing at him because I knew he had overdone it, but he wanted to make sure that he would not disappoint his babies. In his heart he felt as if he'd already disappointed them enough. I gave him his meds and a bottle of water; he took his pills and reclined on the bed. I laid down next to him and he pulled me close and held me in his arms.

I looked in his eyes and told him that I was so happy that he was here. I told him that I was so scared because I thought we were gonna lose him. He said, "I know baby. Thank God, I'm still here." I kissed him and said, "Yes my love, I'm so thankful." I relaxed and after about 20 minutes his medication started to kick in. I studied his face and saw the scars from the accident. I was so grateful to have him right there with me and I was looking forward to going to sleep and waking up with him. Robert seemed to be so peaceful in my arms. The feeling of having him with me was indescribable.

As he lay there in his medication induced sleep, I whispered a prayer of thanks to God. "Lord, it's me Marissa, and I just wanted to thank you for allowing him to live. I know that we are not living in the ideal situation, but I have to stop and give thanks because I know the only reason that Robert is still with us is because of you. Lord please forgive us for our wrongs and help us to make things right." I began to cry because I knew that only God was responsible for Robert and my children being alive. I promised God that I was going to do everything to make sure that we got things right.

My relationship with Robert isn't the perfect relationship and our story is not the perfect one, but it is ours. I can say it until I am blue in the face that I didn't intend for this to happen, but to everyone I'll still be that woman who had babies by a married man. I'll always be the homewrecker.

Loving Robert has been a roller-coaster ride of various emotions. There were times that on one hand I was so guilt stricken and ashamed for being with him but on the other hand I needed him and couldn't breathe without him. I hated myself at times because I felt like I messed up another woman's life. One thing I have realized is that no one can ever take anyone from you. If the person that you are with steps out, they do it because they want to. No person can force anyone to cheat. It's a choice. Making the choice to cheat in many cases happens in a split second and once you're caught up its hard to find your way out. I will not say that everyone who cheats is a bad person, because good people sometimes make bad choices. Neither Robert or myself ever cheated in previous relationships but look at our situation…look at how we came to be.

Robert has given me three beautiful children and he loves them as much as I do. You can't control who you love, how you love, and you definitely can't control when you love. My life will never be the same and neither will Roberts. I can't tell you what the future holds because I don't know, but I do know that as of now, we are in love. We love our children, and we are a family.

All I have ever wanted is for my children to have the life that I didn't have. I want more for them. I am not proud of how I got here with this man that I love so much, but I'm not ashamed of my feelings for him and the reality that we share. I know that there are those who will always stand in judgment of me. People always want to hold you hostage to your mistakes and past, but I don't worry too much about the opinions of others because the truth is that I am not the first and sadly, one thing is certain, I will not be the last.

ABOUT THE AUTHOR

Author Ma'Desa Kinchlow is a native of Indianapolis, IN. She is an author of poetry, and fiction short stories. Ma'Desa began her writing career in 2011 when she launched the Girlfriend Chronicles short story blog. Ma'Desa has a passion and love for the literary and performing arts. This is her debut published book in the Girlfriend Chronicles Series. She currently resides in Phoenix, AZ and is the proud mother of two children.